Corporate Culture and Globalization

This book offers an ethnographic analysis of how corporate culture has been transformed in the age of globalization and promotes the importance of a national ideology's role in corporate culture studies.

Based on 15 months of participant observation as a shop-floor salesperson, this book explores the gap between management-created corporate ideology and employees' interpretations of and responses to this ideology. This book approaches the issue by examining the formation, dissemination, and interpretation of corporate ideology at a global Japanese fashion retailer in Hong Kong. It does so by charting the history of the company's corporate policy: from centralized attempts at corporate employee management, through the creation of store manager "missionaries" intended to disseminate their ideology, to the ultimately unexpected outcomes as corporate ideology collided with its interpretations by store employees.

The interdisciplinary nature of this book will appeal to scholars and upper-level students in the fields of management, marketing, anthropology, and cultural studies as well as those interested in globalization, cross-cultural management, and retail management.

Yi Zhu is a cultural anthropologist based at Lancaster University, UK, specializing in the institutionalization and internalization of culture in the organization, particularly about cultural change and identity negotiation. Her current projects focus on the role of politics in culture change, emotion, and identity work in the organization.

Routledge Advances in Management and Business Studies

Organizational Management and the COVID-19 Crisis
Security and Risk Management Dilemmas
Edited by Wioletta Sylwia Wereda, Jacek Woźniak and Justyna Stochaj

Digital Entrepreneurship and the Global Economy
Edited by J. Mark Munoz

Cross-cultural Knowledge Management
Cultural Influences in China and Brazil
Jacky Hong and Jorge Muniz Jr.

Human Resource Management and Internal Marketing
Teena Mishra

Human Resources Management in Multinational Companies
A Central European Perspective
Marzena Stor

Corporate Culture and Globalization
Ideology and Identity in a Global Fashion Retailer
Yi Zhu

Corporate Compliance and Conformity
A Convenience Theory Approach to Executive Deviance
Petter Gottschalk

For more information about this series, please visit: www.routledge.com/Routledge-Advances-in-Management-and-Business-Studies/book-series/SE0305

Corporate Culture and Globalization

Ideology and Identity in a Global Fashion Retailer

Yi Zhu

Routledge
Taylor & Francis Group
LONDON AND NEW YORK

First published 2023
by Routledge
4 Park Square, Milton Park, Abingdon, Oxon OX14 4RN

and by Routledge
605 Third Avenue, New York, NY 10158

Routledge is an imprint of the Taylor & Francis Group, an informa business

British Library Cataloguing-in-Publication Data
A catalogue record for this book is available from the British Library

Library of Congress Cataloging-in-Publication Data
Names: Zhu, Yi, 1984- author.
Title: Corporate culture and globalization : ideology and identity in a global fashion retailer / Yi Zhu.
Description: Abingdon, Oxon ; New York, NY : Routledge, 2023. | Series: Routledge advances in management and business studies | Includes bibliographical references and index. |
Identifiers: LCCN 2022046542 (print) | LCCN 2022046543 (ebook) | ISBN 9781032304434 (hardback) | ISBN 9781032304441 (paperback) | ISBN 9781003305675 (ebook)
Subjects: LCSH: Corporate culture—Japan—Case studies. | Corporate culture—China—Hong Kong—Case studies. | International business enterprises—Japan—Case studies. | Stores, Retail—China—Hong Kong—Case studies. | Retail trade—China—Hong Kong—Case studies.
Classification: LCC HD58.7 .Z48 2023 (print) | LCC HD58.7 (ebook) | DDC 302.3/5—dc23/eng/20221021
LC record available at https://lccn.loc.gov/2022046542
LC ebook record available at https://lccn.loc.gov/2022046543

ISBN: 978-1-032-30443-4 (hbk)
ISBN: 978-1-032-30444-1 (pbk)
ISBN: 978-1-003-30567-5 (ebk)

DOI: 10.4324/9781003305675

Typeset in Bembo
by codeMantra

To my partner, Donald, my family, HKU friends, and people from Ichi, who helped me create this book.

Contents

Illustrations

Figures

Tables

1 Introduction

I was surprised and nervous yet excited when I was first approached by an academic colleague of mine to ask whether I would be interested in co-teaching a course on business culture at the Japanese headquarters of a Japanese fashion retailer, here called Ichi.[1] This is the company in which I carried out my long-term participant observations as a retail salesperson for my doctoral degree, which is the foundation of this book. I was curious about what happened to the company after I formally left the front-line retail shops and finished my fieldwork. I heard the news about the company from the media and follow-up interviews with employees in the later years; however, I have never really had the feeling of being an insider. As an anthropologist, my goal is to explore the culture of an organization from an insider's perspective without compromising the objectivity and criticality required of a researcher. I thought having this lecturing opportunity may guide me in how I should update my doctoral book and provide an understanding of the company that I explored a few years ago. From the first time I had a meeting with Ichi employees to discuss the lecture contents to the most recent training sessions with global employees, I was convinced that what I observed back then still applies in the current organization. Since my fieldwork, their business has expanded to more overseas markets and their financial performance has improved. However, the topics of this book – embedded corporate ideology, its expression through the organizational system, and policies, as well as identities of employees – are still relevant. I would like to take you through a journey of mine that started in the summer of 2010 and continued for almost one and a half years of "working" as a salesperson at the retail shops of Ichi. My story begins with the opening of a flagship store of Ichi in Hong Kong, aiming to show the importance of the company in Hong Kong from both a Japanese and local perspective.

On a rainy Friday in April, I attended the opening ceremony for the flagship store of Ichi in Hong Kong. On the previous day, I learned from a Japanese store manager that the founder of the company, Takahiro Sakai, would attend the opening ceremony, and his speech would begin at 9 a.m. I then heard that the person in charge of the store, a Hong Kong local, had been replaced by a Japanese manager because the local staff doubted his ability for

DOI: 10.4324/9781003305675-1

the position. I was quite excited to attend the ceremony to see the founder in person since I have only 'seen' him on TV or read about him in books. I immediately called a Japanese university student, Tanaka, who studied at the same university as me to ask if he was interested in joining me. He was excited to hear of the coming of Sakai since he was fascinated by Sakai's management philosophy, a philosophy that challenges the so-called "traditional" Japanese management system and aims toward building a global company.

As it was raining on the morning of the opening ceremony, I took an umbrella and walked toward the bus station to get to the nearest metro station. When I got off the metro at 8:37 a.m., I got a text message from Tanaka saying that he had already arrived. It was raining heavily when I saw Tanaka in front of the store. I found several Ichi employees were preparing for the ceremony and only two reporters were in attendance, so we were able to secure a place quite close to the speech stage. Tanaka told me that the speech began at 9:30 a.m. I later saw four to five customers who appeared to be mainland Chinese line up in front of the store and receive paper fans with Ichi's logo from the staff.

At 9:00 a.m., more reporters arrived, and a member of Ichi's staff asked us to move out of the press area since it had been secured exclusively for the media. We found a place nearby. As we waited for the founder to arrive, I saw a woman from the mainland who works for the Greater China area greeting local employees with a smile and a bow. Several minutes later, Sakai arrived in a red Lexus that was escorted by a white car. Sakai was wearing a suit and was surrounded by flashing cameras. He was shorter than I expected.

Sakai went inside the store, and we soon heard more camera flashes from behind as reporters took photos of a local middle-aged couple. When Tanaka and I discussed the identity of that mysterious couple, I bumped into the wife of a Japanese supervisor who was sent to Ichi Hong Kong. I greeted her and learned that the couple might be the landlords of the property on which the flagship store was located. After the landlords entered the store, Sakai exchanged business cards with them and introduced Zhang Peng, the CEO of Ichi Hong Kong, to them through an interpreter.

Although the ceremony was supposed to start at 9:30 a.m., I saw Sakai continue his conversation with the couple, even though Zhang had reminded him of the time. Around this time, the reporters were taking photos of customers who had lined up and were asking them to wave paper fans. Moreover, the number of reporters had significantly increased by this time. Five minutes later, Sakai came out and the female master of ceremonies, who wore Ichi products, started to introduce the guests. She began with the founder who stood in the middle, then from Sakai's right to left she introduced Zhang Peng, the Consul-General of Japan in Hong Kong, the landlord couple, and the Japanese store manager of the flagship store.

After speeches by Sakai and the Japanese store manager and the ribbon-cutting ceremony, the store opened to customers as reporters took photos. I heard a loud greeting of "Welcome to the store" from smiling employees who stood in a line. I found a familiar face among them, an employee who was highly proficient in the practice of Ichi's unique style of customer service. Several minutes later, I heard concentrated flashes near the entrance where I found a customer asking Sakai to autograph a Chinese translation of Sakai's biography. Tanaka was eager to get Sakai's autograph, so we waited for the opportunity. When Tanaka got an opportunity, he told Sakai in Japanese, "President (*shachō*), I will do my best to bring the operation of Ichi in Europe to another level and to make it the best among overseas markets if I am lucky enough to enter Ichi in the near future." After hearing Tanaka's exciting words, Sakai gave him his business card, tapped Tanaka's shoulder, and said, "After you return to Japan, contact me anytime."

After this exciting moment, we walked around the store. I saw a number of Japanese people who might have been senior executives or important guests checking out this newly opened store, likely trying to figure out why the Hong Kong stores have achieved such high annual sales. Although a relatively small number of customers came by that morning, when I re-visited the store at around 6:00 p.m. on the same day, there were numerous customers in the store and a long queue at the cash counters. Although I bumped into several employees I knew while walking around the store, most of the employees were new. When I walked around near the entrance, I overheard two Japanese staff, who had worked for Ichi Japan saying that the opening day sales target might be surpassed soon.

I went outside the store where I saw a passing tram with an Ichi advertisement on it. It was rare for Ichi to put on an advertisement to be featured on the tram; however, there was the ad on several trams. In addition to the advertising blitz, Ichi also offered free ferry rides on the opening day as part of its promotional campaign. One of my friends who rode the ferry that day appreciated the free ride and heard many local passengers praise Ichi as a company that contributed to local society.

The above description reflects the fact that although Ichi had entered the market eight years ago, the opening of the flagship store still attracted wide media coverage and customers. I also noticed that the visibility of the founder has increased in Hong Kong because of the publication of the Chinese version of his biography and his high ranking on the list of Forbes billionaires in recent years. In Japan, Ichi is a powerful recruiter because many Japanese university students like Tanaka are attracted by its global character and the founder's strong ideology. Along with its increasing presence in Japan and the global market, Ichi has been widely studied particularly by journalists and industry specialists. How did the company gain such achievements? What was the role of the founder in creating the company? Why did Ichi choose Hong Kong, and how will the local subsidiary develop? How does the company manage its employees? How do local employees and Japanese expatriates react to Ichi's management in Hong Kong?

This book represents an anthropological study to address the formation and expression and employees' interpretations of corporate ideology in Ichi

Hong Kong. It examines how Ichi uses its corporate ideology, which has been heavily influenced by the founder's philosophy and the company's historical development, to build the company. This corporate ideology is expressed in the form of a corporate system of training, ranking, remuneration, and promotion. Furthermore, this research shows the manipulation of corporate ideology by employees for their own interests and the transformation of human relations based on various interpretations by Store Managers.

To understand the basic underlying issues explored in previous papers, this chapter starts with a review of the literature on Ichi to point out the unbalanced approach of the research on Ichi. I then cover the development of studies on the corporate ideology that leads us to the widely explored concept of "Japanese management" and *nihonjinron* (theory of Japanese). Critiques of these arguments then follow, to bring to light the importance of anthropological research in studying Japanese organizations.

Many non-academic books and articles focusing on Ichi have been published with an unbalanced approach in the sense that these pieces either appraise only Ichi's legend or overzealously focus on how the company earns profits by mistreating employees.[2]

There have been dozens of books written by journalists that focus on Ichi's business operations or the founder's philosophy. Most books written by former or current Ichi employees were published after the company was recognized as a major brand. The trend in research on Ichi has moved from appraising the company to the founder's rise, biography, and criticism of his approach. From 1999 until 2003, the number of books about Ichi has increased along with its achievements. There were a number of books and articles published when the company received intense media attention because of its high-growth rate, but these publications considerably declined along with the company's decreasing sales. The first autobiography of Ichi's founder was published in 2006, and it has been reprinted 26 times in the past six years. Sakai was regarded as a new breed of a great manager and media coverage encouraged businesspeople to learn from the founder's venture spirit. In 2009 and 2010, there were 14 books about Ichi's success story and corporate system.

Research has shifted to focus on the workers' point of view from the 2011 publication of a book that revealed how Ichi enforced overtime work at low pay for overseas employees. Ichi sued the publisher of this book for defamation, and the lawsuit was ongoing at the end of 2012. This trial was widely covered by the media but there were few articles examining whether Ichi followed a similar practice in Japan or other markets. Subsequently, an article published in a representative Japanese business magazine claimed that the company had, unreasonable work requirements and overtime work, and as a result, had an excessively high attrition rate and a high number of employees who were diagnosed with depression. Publication of the article fueled criticism of Ichi, targeting the founder, who defended the company's practices.

These publications are important for understanding the corporate structure of Ichi and its development history; however, they tend to either propagandize or criticize only superficial aspects of the founder's philosophy instead of its actual practice. They are written from a generalist's point of view and are largely unable to provide readers a glimpse into the core principles of the company – its corporate ideology. There was a book about Ichi written by a journalist who took an "undercover" approach aiming to expose the reality of working at Ichi that detailed the nature of its work culture. The journalist worked as a salesperson for about a year at retail shops in Japan. By comparing our books, I found many similarities in terms of the observations we made at the store such as how people identify themselves to the company and how the organization manages employees. However, our books differ because while the journalist's book aimed to expose unethical practices in an organization, I aimed to explain the cultural logic of management in the organization. It is more about how to understand the phenomenon rather than attempting to pass judgment on its practices. I believe academic research could level out the unbalanced approach to organization; moreover, corporate ethnography could offer readers a detailed analysis of the corporate ideology and people within the organization.

Before moving into the literature of corporate ethnography, I will review how the company's corporate ideology has been studied over time by scholars of organizational studies and how the *nihonjinron* has emerged as a result of the search for the "myth" of the Japanese company's success.

Corporate Ideology and *Nihonjinron*

Research on organizational study began when the publication of Max Weber's seminal work was established. He argues subjectivity of individuals forms the pattern of social organization and that people's behaviors and interactions have a distinct relationship with specific cultural contexts. In the same vein as Weber's viewpoint, the modernist perspective or rationalist approach could be regarded as the starting point of the field of organizational study. This approach has been adopted by scholars trying to discover the fundamentals of organizational rationality and the relationship between formal structure and informal forms (Moeran, 2013: 3). Scholars examine the systematic nature of the organizations, particularly bureaucracies, which have been the subject of numerous studies on organizational design.

Subsequently, scholars started to put members of organizations at the center of their research on organizational culture, leadership, and management, and scholars attempted to examine the general picture of the structure and function of organizations based on empirical data. The emergence of study of issues of decision-making and choice within an organization also emerged at the same time (Simon, 1976). Studies by sociologists and anthropologists started to receive more attention within the field, and many scholars in management studies began to focus on the culture within organizations. Culture is now considered as a possible candidate to explain varied organizational behaviors and levels of stability in groups (Ouchi, 1981; Schein, 1990).

The issue of culture within organizations became the focus of scholars, and this trend intensified with the economic boom in Japan from the 1970s to the early 1980s, when Japan had a growing presence in the world, as the economic situation in some Western countries, especially the U.S., was unfavorable. During this time, management scholars tried to identify the answer to the "Japanese miracle" by studying the cultural aspects of Japanese business and the crucial element of underlying ideology (Moeran, 2013: 13). Scholars in management studies conducted much research on Japanese companies and concluded that it was the "distinctive" features of Japanese culture that allowed Japanese companies to succeed.

The study of the Japanese miracle prompted the emergence of the *nihonjinron*, which stresses the idea that the cultural distinctions inherent in Japanese culture are the most influential factors in the country's business success (Abegglen, 1956, 1973; Christopher, 1983; Curtis, 1969; Drucker, 1971; Gibney, 1998; Ouchi, 1981; Reischauer, 1977; Vogel, 1979). Literature related to *nihonjinron* claims that industrial familialism, represented by harmonious worker relations, a focus on workers' welfare, collectivism, and so on, has formed the ideology of the Japanese company. Most of the literature on this subject reaches these conclusions after merely looking at the superficial, represented picture of companies. In addition, before the high-growth era, early studies and research on Japanese companies were dominated by negative evaluations. In the 1960s, the Japanese management hierarchy was widely criticized by scholars for its paternalistic system and the inefficiency of the *ringi* system (see Yoshino, 1968).

Prompted by post-war economic growth in Japan, Peter F. Drucker (1971) published an influential paper that proposed three important agenda items for American firms. Drucker states that although the consensus building required by *ringi* takes time, it becomes efficient once achieved. The second is that higher productivity is achieved under the *ringi* system because it provides the psychological comforts of lifetime employment and lifetime training. The last idea proposed by Drucker is that training by informal *senpai-kohai* (fraternal) relationships results in highly effective top management.

The work of James Abegglen is a representative case, showing how scholars' arguments have changed along with the economic climate in Japan. Abegglen published "*The Japanese Factory*" (1956) and claims that the Japanese employment system has similar characteristics to earlier Japan and pre-industrial times, distinct from the Western pattern. In Chapter 7, he criticizes the "lifetime commitment" and "seniority-based payment" in Japanese companies, which have given rise to inefficiencies and reduced productivity.

Although Abegglen initially criticized the Japanese management system and how it has been largely shaped by Japanese culture, in the revised edition of his book released in 1973, entitled "*Management and worker: the Japanese solution*", the negative chapter has been completely removed, and replaced by a chapter praising the Japanese culture's influence on organizations. This change was made after witnessing Japan's high-growth economy. Since Abegglen's seminal work, scholars in management studies have widely pointed to the "unique" cultural characteristics of Japan to explain the country's achievements. This phenomenon has expanded to the Japanese government. Masao Matsunaga, the Deputy Minister of Health, Labor, and Welfare wrote in the preface of the government's official labor report in 1972 that lifetime employment (*shōgai koyō*), seniority-based pay (*nenkō chingin*), and enterprise union (*kigyō betsu kumiai*) are the three pillars of the "Japanese employment system (*nihon teki koyō seido*)" (Takahashi, 2010: 99).

Countering research done by Abegglen, Ronald Dore attempts to explain the origin of the unique Japanese employment system by citing the social democratic revolution in Japan in his 1973 book, "*British Factory-Japanese Factory: The origins of national diversity in industrial relations*". He argues that there is an increasing convergence between Japanese- and British-style organizations. He cites factors that Abegglen did not focus much on, such as worker relations, differences between permanent and temporary workers, and gender issues in the workplace. Dore's approach is unique in that he explains the origin of Japanese business culture not only from the contemporary point of view but also in terms of the pre-war period. Dore concludes that characteristics of the Japanese employment system, such as the distant relationship between foreman and worker, distinctions between permanent and temporary workers, and collective responsibility are actually greatly influenced by the feudal period (1973: 401).

Thomas Rohlen (1974) conducted fieldwork in a Japanese bank to explore the characteristics of harmony and loyalty by male salaried men in the organization. Rohlen finds that loyalty to the office was similar to the farmer's importance in the household, and employees' loyalty follows the same pattern as the farmer's loyalty to the community. He also points to examples of spiritual training for recruits, through a welcome ceremony and a ritual company song, in attempting to explain how employees develop a sense of community. Louella Matsunaga claims that Rohlen's and similar analyses have a link to Anderson's (1991) research that suggests employees who have never met could create an "imagined community" (Matsunaga, 2000: 4).

"Japaneseness" has been emphasized by the above scholars to explain the harmonious and bounded organizations of Japan, most suggesting that Western countries should learn from the Japanese way of management. Since the 1980s, some scholars in the field of management studies argue that this theory overemphasizes cultural aspects and neglects the rationality behind company practices. Scholars such as Kazuo Koike (1984, 1995) and Masahiko Aoki (1986, 1990, 1991, 1992) have published a number of articles claiming the distinctive feature of the Japanese employment system is rooted in an economic perspective.

Koike's examination of blue-collar workers in large steel factories in the U.S. and Japan shows that Japanese blue-collar workers have a greater degree of autonomy on the shop floor and develop their intellectual skills by deployment and promotion more than their U.S. counterparts (1984: 48).

Koike concludes that while Japanese workers have experience working in almost all positions in the workshop through an egalitarian job rotation, U.S. workers have lost mobility. This deployment system indicates that seniority is less important in Japanese workshops than it is in U.S. shops. As a result, skilled Japanese workers can contribute more to the workshop based on their wide range of skills (1984: 67). In his work, Koike claims that seniority-based compensation is common for Western white-collar workers; however it is unique to Japanese firms regarding its extension to blue-collar workers (1995: 263).

Aoki criticizes the simple cultural explanation of the so-called Japanese employment system and states that firms are complex organizations that operate rationally. Aoki examines two information structures in U.S. and Japanese firms to provide a theoretical framework for comparisons between an industrial organization in the U.S. and Japan (1986: 971). He claims that the U.S. system has a vertical hierarchy and the Japanese one is horizontal in the sense that job classifications in the U.S. are more specialized than those in Japan. The U.S. system tries to manage employees by a rational hierarchical control, while the Japanese system is more ambiguous and dependent on on-site workers to cope with emergent events (1986: 972). The second point Aoki stresses is that Japanese workers on-site communicate without the intervention of a supervisor (1986: 972). Aoki offers an alternative way to explain the nature of Japanese firms by employing economic reasoning, based on the rationality principle (1991: 5).

We could infer from the research of *nihonjinron* that there might be cultural influences on the management of Japanese companies; however, we cannot look into the cultural aspect in isolation when we study companies as profit-making centers. The literature of Japanese economists has permitted us to pay attention to the rational aspect of company systems. However, both research approaches have failed to disclose the full picture of corporate ideology since it is not possible to confirm whether the corporate ideology is practiced in reality, as companies have claimed without direct observation by researchers.

Certain groups of scholars have pointed to the importance of the individual and divisive human relations in Japanese organizations to avoid an unbalanced portrayal of Japan, particularly after the collapse of the bubble economy (Graham, 2003: 11). Moeran points out scholars of *nihonjinron* have fallen into the trap of confusing family ideology with its actual practice (Moeran, 2013: 17). Alvesson also claims that it is important to study various components inside companies rather than focusing on the overall organization itself (1993).

I will, therefore, look into how researchers who have criticized the over-simplification of *nihonjinron* reveal conflicted human relations inside Japanese firms rather than harmonious ones, the gap between ideology and its actual practice, and so on, based on observations inside various Japanese companies.

Ethnographies of the Japanese Company

"Anti-*nihonjinron*" literature has emerged since the methodology used by Japanologists over-simplified the fact that every Japanese company has distinctive features and does not fall under an overarching type of management. Ethnographic studies written by scholars, including Clark (1979), Fruin (1983), Noguchi (1990), Kondo (1990), Hamabata (1990), Wong (1999), Matsunaga (2000), Graham (2003), and Sedgwick (2003) have contributed to the deconstruction of the simple cultural explanation.

Rodney Clark in his book suggests an alternative explanation regarding how to understand Japanese companies in terms of cultural and market orientation (Clark, 1979). He thoroughly examines the historical background of a large Japanese firm and the relationship between the company and the broader society without neglecting a market analysis. Clark describes the historical background of the development of the Japanese company, and he investigates how Japanese companies play a role as a single unit of the industrial organization by examining the relationship between Japanese companies and their surrounding environment. His research offers us another angle from which to study the Japanese company.

Mark Fruin (1983) who studied a Japanese *shōyu* (soy sauce) company explains that the introduction of "Japanese-style" personnel management started during the 1920s and 1930s when "a new system of paternalism that wedded two seemingly unsuited partners: corporate welfare and corporate productivity" emerged (Fruin, 1983: 224). Fruin offers an example of the unequal distribution of benefits under paternalism between full-timers and temporary workers and claims that these practices were not modeled on traditional ties of "warmth and affection" between masters and workers in Tokugawa times. He also attacks the myth that such "warm and affectionate" relationships existed at all.

In Noguchi's (1990) study of the Japanese national railways, he aims to provide a critical examination of the conventional study of Japanese organizations, focusing on the issues of industrial familialism and the lifetime employment system, which are seen as crucial elements of the Japanese organization. He argues that these observations hide the ongoing picture of workers by suggesting that different categories of workers have differing attitudes toward industrial familialism, which results in conflicts between them (1990: 3). Noguchi stresses that so-called industrial harmony or familialism is in fact "a corporate ideology based on the superficial public relations image that an organization presents to society" (1990: 4).

The above three research studies allow us to view a new picture of Japanese corporate organizations based on fieldwork. They are similar in that they tend to focus more on male full-time workers in large Japanese organizations. In order to understand the Japanese company as a whole, scholars have gradually shifted their research context to different kinds of organizations and workers, particularly since the 1990s (Graham, 2003). Increasing attention has been paid to temporary workers and female informants as opposed to full-time salaried men (see Hamabata, 1990; Kondo, 1990; Matsunaga, 2000). These researches paint a picture of how "peripheral" groups of companies within the society and employees within these organizations were represented.

Matsunaga (2000), who conducted research on a Japanese retailer in Japan asks if the so-called Japanese employment system can still survive the economic changes in Japan. Through fieldwork, she concludes that the changing Japanese economy has a strong influence on the ideology of the company as a community. She discusses the boundary between the company and counterparts and finds that the ability of employees to distinguish themselves from customers is permeable (Matsunaga, 2000: 172). She notes that along with the changing Japanese economy, the view of the company as a community also needs to be revised (Matsunaga, 2000: 176). Matsunaga's research allows us to pay attention to the groups of employees that received little attention in earlier studies and to reconsider our past analysis of Japanese companies through the lens of economic change. From her work, we do not derive a clear picture of how Store Managers who are the "soul" of the retail company have contributed to forming human relations within a store.

The above-referenced literature failed to mention neither how Japanese companies have operated in overseas markets nor how they have managed local employees. Since the late 1990s, some scholars have focused on company managerial practices abroad, among them the work of Wong (1999), Sedgwick (2007), and Kishi (2009) are representative. These studies contribute to our understanding of the typical Japanese company's managerial control abroad and how Japanese expatriates interact with local employees in the context of the Japanese company as a whole.

Heung Wah Wong's work (1999) helps us to understand how a Japanese regional supermarket has transformed its business format in Hong Kong and how the company managed employees within the context of the company's ideology and a dual structure that placed Japanese workers in superior positions over local employees. His research is valuable in the sense that it allows us to understand how current Japanese firms such as Ichi have shifted their managerial strategy to stress the ambition of 'globalization' although Ichi differed from the company studied in Wong's work in terms of the number of Japanese expatriates, historical and economical background, and the company's position in Japan and the world.

Mitchell Sedgwick (2007) challenges anthropology's general approach to globalization, based on his anthropological analysis of cross-cultural social interactions inside a Japanese consumer electronics multinational, YamaMax in France. Sedgwick interacted primarily with technical personnel within the company, and his ethnography provides us with a new picture of specialists inside the Japanese company; however, this work has not fully reported on front-line workers who played a significant role in company operations.

Yasuyuki Kishi (2009) analyzes employee training in a Japanese electronics firm in Taiwan from cultural and social perspectives based on his observations. His specific focus is on Taiwanese higher-ranked employees who have many years of service in the company and their attempts to find their role within the organization. Kishi points out that these Taiwanese managers gain important cultural adaptations for surviving in the Japanese organization such as becoming fluent in Japanese, patience, collectivism, and thoroughness based on their years of service, and long-term training and interactions with Japanese counterparts (2009). Kishi calls these Taiwanese managers "cultural mediators" who play the role of a bridge between Japanese expatriates and local employees (2009). His book is valuable to our understanding of the role of local employees within Japanese organizations abroad; however, his research contains little data on how local employees interpret the corporate ideology and what drives them to become "cultural mediators".

While much anthropological and sociological research on Japanese companies has been conducted, management studies scholars who used to appraise the "Japanese management" have tended to criticize its efficacy, claiming that the cultural aspect of the Japanese company has resulted in an ethnocentric management approach and limited localization and contributed to the long-term recession of the Japanese economy. Kopp (1994) argued that Japanese companies are ethnocentric in the sense that they place a higher number of expatriates in top management positions in overseas subsidiaries when compared to Western counterparts. Other scholars say that although the number of expatriates might be limited, the transfer of authority to the local level should be increased (see Hu, 2003; Huruta, 2004; Legewie, 2000; Seki and Han, 2003; Yahagi, 2007).

The above scholars conducted research as "outsiders" and their conclusions seem to rely heavily on the economic situation of the country or the particular company. Nobuo Takahashi (2010) points out that the core parts of Japanese management philosophy have, in fact, changed little. Moreover, the pattern of success by one particular company might not get the same result when applied to another one since it is employees and their various career orientations, personal traits, and so on, who carry out company operations. Problems of methodology plagued the above scholars and prevented them from discovering how employees feel toward the subject companies' managerial decisions and practices.

A company's managerial direction and methods are largely influenced by its corporate ideology, which is continuously adjusting to the internal and external environment of the company. During the process of change, employees might react in different ways toward the company and behave in various ways to secure their interests. In the next section, I will discuss the major theoretical framework of my book in terms of the process of a company building in the face of a changing corporate ideology and the reaction by employees.

Company-Building Process

Literature on nation-building offers hints on how to examine the process of company building, which is similar to nation-building in the sense that it is a corporate ideology that largely influences the direction of company development and its managerial practices in addition to external factors. To build an "integrated" company, it is necessary to "identify" its unique corporate ideology. The process of instilling this ideology requires a certain period of time for employees within the company to regard its ideology as something "unquestionable" and natural; otherwise, the corporate ideology might be ineffective in achieving company goals.

Orvar Lofgren defines the process of national culture formation as a "cultural praxis of national identity formation" (1989: 5). According to the view presented by Richard Fox (1990) nations as cultural products, and nationalism is a cultural process of collective identity formation, much literature has explored how intellectuals and political elites have formed a distinctive national culture to build up their nation. As Richard Handler proposes, the key lesson of nation-building is that even though individual members within a nation differ in various aspects, their shared attributes allow them to form a national identity and this sameness overrides differences (1985: 6).

The process of creating a national culture requires the identification of a distinctive feature that separates outsiders and insiders. Foster argues that national culture does not only forge a national identity, but it is "the naturalization of arbitrariness" (1991: 237). LiPuma and Meltzoff (1990) examine the cultural transformation of the Solomon Islands. They address how the indigenous elite in the central government of the Solomon Islands have formed its public culture. The elite creates a national public sphere and a public culture to forge a common identity and to make it "appear to be real, unquestionable, and an intrinsic element of personal identity" (LiPuma and Meltzoff, 1990: 89). The national elite not only constructed an external national identity but also an internal one to build up their own culture in the eyes of new Solomon Islands citizens who were defined by and respond to this national identity.

Durkheim has claimed that the function of religious collective representations is similar to the rites and symbols of nationhood (cited in Foster, 1991: 239) and communities have been constructed with internal classifications and external environments. Richard Feinberg (1986), who has examined the creation of a sense of national identity in a place called Anuta, a small isolated island in the eastern Solomons, shows how nationalist elites use rites and symbols to build up a sense of shared national identity and highlight the problem of "integration".

Foster in his work cites Kapferer's (1988, 1989) use of the word 'ontology' to explain the formalized character of ideologies in his comparative study of two nationalist ideologies (1991: 254). Kapferer identifies the hierarchical system of Sinhalese Buddhist nationalist ideology and juxtaposes this with egalitarian Australian nationalist ideology to point out these differing conceptions of society and how they result in very different nations. According to Kapferer, while Australian nationalist ideology places an emphasis on the autonomy of human beings, Sinhalese Buddhist nationalist ideology emphasizes a fractured society and hence nation. Foster adds that "society is either an extension of the individual's natural autonomy (a collective individual), threatened by the impositions of the state or the enabling condition of ideal personhood, dependent upon the state's power to encompass difference within the hierarchy" (1991: 254).

Eric Wolf (1956) claims that nations must "possess cultural forms or mechanisms which groups involved in the same overall web of relationships can use in their formal and informal dealings with each other" (1065–1078). Wolf (1958) examines how the Virgin of Guadalupe forms a Mexican national system based on the examination of "how the cultural idiom of behaviors and ideal representations through which different groups of the same society can pursue and manipulate their different fates within a coordinated framework" (34). Wolf claims that the Guadalupe symbol provides a cultural framework for expressing the "collective representation" of Mexican society (1958: 38).

Foster (1991) claims that nation-building is a continuously changing process and there are many different and influential factors that prompt a nation to maintain its "imagined community". Foster writes:

> Neither the nation-as-community nor, therefore, national culture has any essential properties... Nations, and national cultures are artifacts-continually imagined, invented, contested, and transformed by the agencies of individual persons, the state, and global flows of commodities. As an ideology, nationalism (as well as a set of correlated practices, the nation) is perhaps the most compelling and consequential artifact of modern times. But it is nonetheless an artifact, formulated variously, with various effects, in various social and historical contexts.
>
> Foster (1991: 252)

Just like the dichotomy of nation-building separates the political elite or state officials from people within nations, Ichi's similar dichotomy is manifested in the separation of the Head Office and stores. At Ichi, to build a company as an "integrated" and "bounded" organization, office employees must identify and formulate a corporate ideology that includes spiritual values and material rewards and inculcates this into store employees as something they "possess". Some scholars point out employees can manipulate and respond to a corporate ideology based on their individual interests; therefore, it is crucial in Ichi's case to "monitor" whether the corporate ideology "successfully" turns into something that employees take for granted. The means used by nations to implement a national identity vary and include cultural activities, political systems, and so on, and this is similar to the case of building a company ideology.

Methodology

As this book intends to explore the institutional culture of Ichi, it is necessary to discuss why anthropological research based on fieldwork is needed to achieve this goal. As Barth (1969) describes, "culture is nothing but a way to describe human behavior". Culture is not fixed but its process is a circle connecting representation, identity, production, consumption, and regulation (Paul du Gay et al., 1997).

Of the various methodologies, anthropological research conducted through long-term fieldwork has most influenced our understanding of the organizational nature of culture (Moeran, 2013: 2). In-depth participant observation allows researchers to understand human behaviors beyond the corporate ideology to gain a broader picture of the institutional culture of Ichi. The ethnographic approach has allowed us to illuminate and provide a rich understanding of specific organizational phenomena and it could help us build a better theory (Barley, 1983; Schein, 1990; Van Maanen, 1988). Ethnography requires "thick description" as Geertz claims (1973: 5) so that direct observation is the preferred research method.

Although it might be possible to "observe" human relations from outside, this approach may prevent us from understanding the distinctions between what subjects *say* and what they actually *feel*. During fieldwork, researchers encountered numerous occasions in which subjects complained about their subordinates or colleagues to try to justify their own status. However, researchers found that these same subjects behaved in contrast to their statements, showing a completely different picture of the workplace. In an organization such as a company, researchers were given the opportunity to meet various employees with different educational and family backgrounds and observe the different faces they displayed on various occasions. It was quite hard for researchers to divide the subjects into specific categories and connect coherent pieces together. During the classification process, researchers must understand the difference between what people *say* they do, which reflects their justifications, and what they *actually* do, which shows in their behavior in practice. The two might differ drastically.

Researchers are able to take a broad view when they examine the changes between employees and organizations by conducting fieldwork (Moeran, 2005). This advantage results in finding the connections between unrelated aspects and permits the use of data to understand dynamics at work in general, which differentiates fieldwork-based research from the work of scholars in management schools, especially in terms of data analysis.

It is not sufficient to observe human behavior over a short time period since corporate ideology and group boundaries within the corporate structure might change along with internal and external factors, as these boundaries are also subjective and continuously negotiated among people. Kondo (1990) argues that culture is a process and a system of negotiated meanings rather than an absolute.

To study a company from an anthropological point of view, I first needed to find a company that would accept my request. I was lucky enough to be accepted by Ichi as an intern[3] for conducting my fieldwork from August 2010 until December 2011. I had access to three different stores, although I spent most of my fieldwork, for the year beginning in August 2010, at the

East Point City (EPC) store located on East Kowloon Island, Hong Kong. At the end of 2010, I had the opportunity to work as a helper for one day before the opening day of the store and its first day in Kowloon Bay, which allowed me to experience the tense atmosphere of the opening. During my final three months of fieldwork, I gained the opportunity to work as a helper at the Taikoo store. The basic shift was eight hours a day and five days a week, which was similar to the schedules of full-time employees, although I was in general not required to work overtime. Because of the government scholarship that I received during my study period, I did not have an employment contract with the company nor get any payment for my work.

Although the fieldwork period made was not easy, the "company hunting" process was also difficult. In the first year of my degree program, I was busy with school and field work "hunting". Since I am a newcomer to Hong Kong from Japan, where I have lived for more than 12 years in total, I had to make the connection for my fieldwork so attended various gatherings, particularly events organized by the university Old Boys (OB) associations. To gain contact with candidate companies, I joined not only my own alumni network but also the clubs of some other private universities. After every gathering, I sent e-mails to the *senpai* (senior students), who were mostly Japanese expatriates in large commercial firms and banks, to ask for help. Although I had not received any positive replies for several months, I continued my "social life" of attending OB events. I also identified possible companies and contacted the Japanese Head Office and local branches, although none of them replied to me except the Head Office of Ichi.[4]

In the summer of 2010, a president of a university OB association asked me if I was interested in getting to know one of his former subordinates, Yamada, who had his own firm in Hong Kong. Yamada ran a human resources company and his office was incidentally in the same building as Ichi's. I was not expecting anything before I met Yamada, since I was told quite often that it was hard to find a firm that would accept my "special" identity. During the conversation with the president of the OB association and Yamada, I happened to know that Yamada had business with Ichi, and he was willing to introduce me to the head of Ichi's Human Resources Department.

I was able to meet the Director of the Human Resources Department, Mary, several days later with my proposal and resume written in English. I was afraid that Mary might ask me to speak either Cantonese or English, but I was relieved after hearing her fluent Mandarin. We discussed my research plan in the back room of an Ichi store and she asked me many questions such as what particularly I was interested in regarding Ichi and what drove me to choose the company. After scanning my documents, she commented that the content of my proposal was too ambiguous, and she wanted me to bring more detailed versions when we met the Japanese head of the Store Operations Department, Mizuno.

The meeting with Mizuno and Mary was quickly arranged, and we met several days later at the Head Office of Ichi. I brought my revised proposal and resume in both English and Japanese. Mizuno, who was in his late 30s, showed his smile during the meeting and I was surprised to see such a young top manager in a *Japanese* company. Mizuno understood my passion for conducting research on Ichi; however, he repeatedly emphasized that the system in Hong Kong was not a standardized one and the system would be changed within the next few years. Moreover, regarding my request to conduct fieldwork in the Head Office, they seemed to be reluctant, and Mary commented that "there are no special things to observe here". Mizuno and Mary told me that they would contact me later with detailed instructions. Several days later, I received an e-mail informing me that I was assigned to work as an "intern" at the EPC store located in East Kowloon Island, and I was advised to attend one day of training at the Head Office. Before the training was conducted that day, I met Mary and Mark, the Supervisor of my store, to discuss the details regarding my "internship". Mary was worried that the language barrier would cause customer complaints, so Mark gave me a card saying that I would only be available for Japanese and Mandarin customers, which turned out later to be meaningless to local customers.

Through daily work with employees, I have got rich first-hand information for this book, still, there were some limitations to my fieldwork. The first was caused by the language barrier and my mainland Chinese nationality. After several weeks, I was more confident that I understood conversations during daily interactions with local employees, and my mainland Chinese nationality barely influenced my relationship with local employees since most of them regarded me as either Taiwanese or Japanese, whichever they preferred. However, I was always nervous that my identity as a mainland Chinese national might negatively influence the reputation of the store, so I avoided learning some tasks at the store such as taking phone calls since those tasks required more interaction with customers and the more skills I learned, the more tasks I would be assigned, which might result in less time for research observations. Because of these limitations, I was not able to collect sufficient data on these issues.

Another limitation was my fieldwork location. I was basically not "preferred" by the Head Office employees to work at the Head Office since they claimed that there was nothing special to be observed there. Therefore, my research mainly focuses on the store operation, which fails to explore a broader picture of the company as a whole.

Because of the limitation of working at a single store for a relatively long time, I attempt to overcome these limitations by conducting intensive interviews with employees at other stores. I conducted one-on-one interviews with 18 people, including four Japanese expatriates, 12 local employees, and two former employees. Interviews were conducted during my fieldwork and afterward. I did not only target current employees but also those who had resigned. Besides formal interviews, I regularly joined Japanese expatriates for lunch every Wednesday after their English lessons, and I also joined some informal events such as karaoke and barbeques with local employees. Only by building up trust with employees, was this book accomplished, revealing the real, dynamic picture of the store employees' lives at Ichi.

Outline of the Chapters

Chapter 2 addresses how Ichi identified and formulated its corporate ideology – Ichi DNA – based on an examination of the company's historical development and the founder's legacy, to point out the contents and the nature of its distinctive ideology. In Chapter 3, I move on to an examination of the economic background of Ichi and its development in Hong Kong to analyze the contributing factors to the company's early success and how the implementation of its corporate ideology has been aimed to build its company in Hong Kong. In Chapter 4, I describe one day's work at the Ichi store to illustrate work conditions and draw major findings from this book.

Chapters 5 and 6 are dedicated to the examination of how Ichi's building process has been expressed in the form of a corporate system, including its training regimen, ranking of workers, and system of reward. I particularly focus on how the company encourages employees to learn Ichi-specific skills to "inherit" its DNA, under a corporate system that was also used as a means to monitor its progress in building up the company.

The picture of differing interpretations of the corporate ideology by employees is covered in Chapters 7 and 8. In Chapter 7, the book explains the formal promotion system and its informal practice to address how employees behave in sharing their interpretations of the corporate ideology where the examination is focused on the concept of "presentation of self" and collaboration. In Chapter 8, I bring to light the "regimes" of local and Japanese Store Managers who have the power to transform human relations. Rather than their ethnic differences, their various styles of managerial control are most influenced by their interpretation of corporate ideology.

The concluding chapter contributes to the discussion of this book' implications in terms of Ichi's company-building process, how the process is expressed, and different employees' interpretations of Ichi's corporate ideology.

Notes

1 The names of the company and people are fictitious.
2 To avoid revealing the identity of the company, I refrain from citing the source related to Ichi in this book.
3 Internship program for university graduates in Ichi has started half a year after my field work.
4 Ichi staff in Japan wrote me a letter saying that they do not have an internship system; therefore, they could not offer me an opportunity.

References

Abegglen, J. (1956) *The Japanese Factory: Aspects of its Social Organization*. New York: Free Press.

Abegglen, J. (1973) *Management and Worker: The Japanese Solution*. Tokyo: Kodansha.

Anderson, B., & Communities, I. (1991) *Reflections on the Origin and Spread of Nationalism*. London, New York: Political Science.

Aoki, M. (1986) Horizontal Vs. Vertical Information Structure of the Firm. *The American Economic Review*, 76(5), pp. 971–983.

Aoki, M. (1990) Toward an Economic Model of the Japanese Firm. *Journal of Economic Literature,* 28(1), pp. 1–27.

Aoki, M. (1991) Aspects of the Japanese firm. In Aoki, M. (ed.), *The Economic Analysis of the Japanese Firm*, pp. 3–46. Amsterdam; The Netherlands: North Holland.

Aoki, M. (1992) Decentralization-Centralization in Japanese Organization: A dual Principle. In Kumon, S. and Rosovsky, H. (eds.), *The Japanese Political Economy (Vol. 3)*, pp. 142–169. Stanford: Stanford University Press.

Barley, S.R. (1983) Semiotics and the Study of Occupational and Organizational Cultures. *Administrative Science Quarterly*, 28, pp. 393–413.

Barth, F. (1969) *Ethnic Groups and Boundaries: The Social Organization of Culture Difference*. Prospect Heights, IL: Waveland Press, Inc.

Christopher, R.C. (1983) *The Japanese Mind: The Goliath Explained*. New York: Linden Press.

Clark, R. (1979) *The Japanese Company*. Cambridge, MA: Yale University Press.

Curtis, G. (1969) *Election Campaigning, Japanese Style*. New York: Columbia University Press.

Dore, R. (1973) *British Factory-Japanese Factory: The Origins of National Diversity in Industrial Relations*. London: George Allen & Unwin.

Drucker, P.F. (1971) What We Can Learn from Japanese Management. *Harvard Business Review* (Mar-Apr), pp. 110–122.

Du Gay, P. et al. (1997) *Doing Cultural Studies: The Story of the Sony Walkman*. London: Sage Publications.

Feinberg, R. (1986) The 'Anuta Problem': Local Sovereignty and National Integration in the Solomon Islands. *Man*, 21(3), pp. 438–452.

Foster, R.J. (1991) National Cultures in the Global Ecumene. *Annual Review of Anthropology*, 20, pp. 235–260.

Fox, R.G. (eds.) (1990) *Nationalist Ideologies and the Production of National Cultures*. Washington, DC: American Anthropological Association.

Fruin, M.W. (1983*) Kikkoman: Company, Clan, and Community*. Cambridge: Harvard University Press

Geertz, C. (1973) *The Interpretation of Cultures*. New York: Basic.

Gibney, F. (1998) *Unlocking the Bureaucrat's Kingdom: Deregulation and the Japanese Economy*. Washington, DC: Brookings Institution Press.

Graham, F. (2003) *Inside the Japanese Company*. London: Routledge.

Hamabata, M.M. (1990) *Crested Kimono: Power and Love in the Japanese Business Family*. Ithaca, NY: Cornell University Press.

Handler, R. (1985) On Having a Culture: Nationalism and the Preservation of Quebec's Patrimoine. In Stocking, G.W. (eds.), *Objects and Others: Essays on Museums and Material Culture*, pp. 192–217. Madison: University of Wisconsin Press.

Hu, X. (2003) Kokusai kouri kigyo no chugoku senryaku –karuhūru to it ōyōkadō no jirei hikaku [Strategy in China by International Retailers: Comparative Study of Carrefour and Ito-Yokado]. In Yahagi, T. (ed.), *Chūgoku·ajia no kourigyō: zenkyū (gurō baru) ka no inpakuto [Retail Innovation in China and Asia]*, pp. 53–77. Tokyo: Nikkei.

Huruta, A. (2004) *Chugoku ni okeru Nikkei kigyō no keiei genchika. [Managerial Localization by Japanese Companies in China]*. Tokyo: Zeimu Keiri Kyōkai.

Kapferer, B. (1988) *Legends of People, Myths of State: Violence, Intolerance, and Political Culture in Sri Lanka and Australia*. Washington, DC: Smithsonian Institution Press.

Kapferer, B. (1989) Nationalist Ideology and a Comparative Anthropology. *Ethnos*, 54(3–4), pp. 161–199.

Kishi, Y. (2009) *Shain ryoku ha "bunka nōryoku" – Taiwan jin kanbu ga kataru nikkei kigyō no jinzai ikusei. [Ability of Employee is 'Cultural Ability' – Narrative Story of Training Told by Taiwanese Managers]*. Tokyo: Fukyosha.

Koike, K. (1984) Skill Formation Systems in the U.S. and Japan: A Comparative Study. In Aoki, M. (ed.), *The Economic Analysis of the Japanese Firm*, pp.47–75. North-Holland: Elsevier Science Publishers B.V.

Koike, K. (1995) Intellectual Skills and Long-Term Competition. In Imai, K. and Komiya, R. (eds.), *Business Enterprise in Japan: Views of Leading Japanese Economists*, pp. 261–274. Cambridge: The MIT Press.

Kondo, D.K. (1990) *Crafting Selves: Power, Gender and Discourses of Identity in a Japanese Workplace*. Chicago: The University of Chicago Press.

Kopp, R. (1994) *The Rice-Paper Ceiling: Breaking through Japanese Corporate Culture*. Berkeley, CA: Stone Bridge Press.

Legewie, J. (2000) Production Strategies of Japanese Firms: Building Up a Regional Production Network. In Legewie, J. and Meyer-Ohle, H. (eds.), *Corporate Strategies for Southeast Asia after the Crisis*, pp.74–99. Basingstoke: Palgrave.

LiPuma, E., & Meltzoff, S.K. (1990) Ceremonies of Independence and Public Culture in the Solomon Islands. *Public Culture*, 3(1), pp. 77–92.

Lofgren, O. (1989) The Nationalization of Culture. *Ethnologia Europaea*, 19(1), pp. 5–24.

Matsunaga, L. (2000) *The Changing Face of Japanese Retail: Working in a Chain Store*. London: Routledge.

Moeran, B. (2005) *The Business of Ethnography: Strategic Exchanges, People and Organization*. Oxford: Berg.

Moeran, B. (2013) Business Anthropology, Family Ideology and Japan, Chinese. *Journal of Applied Anthropology*, 1(2), pp. 1–22.

Noguchi, P.H. (1990) *Delayed Departures, Overdue Arrivals: Industrial Familiarism and the Japanese National Railway*. Hawaii: University of Hawaii Press.

Ouchi, W.G. (1981) *Theory Z: How American Business can Meet the Japanese Challenge*. Reading: Addison-Wesley.

Reischauer, E. (1977) *The Japanese*. Cambridge: Belknap Press of Harvard University Press.

Rohlen, T.P. (1974) *For Harmony and Strength: Japanese White-Collar Organization in Anthropological Perspective*. Berkeley: University of California Press.

Schein, E.H. (1990) Organizational Culture. *American Psychologist*, 45(2), pp. 109–119.

Schein, E.H., & Bennis, W.G. (1965) *Personal and Organizational Change Through Group Methods*. New York: Wiley.

Sedgwick, M.W. (2003) Positioning "Globalization" at Overseas Subsidiaries of Japanese Multinational Corporations. In Befu, H. and Guichard-Anguis, S. (eds.), *Globalizing Japan*, pp. 65–73. London: Routledge.

Sedgwick, M.W. (2007) *Globalisation and Japanese Organisational Culture: An Ethnography of a Japanese Corporation in France*. London: Routledge.

Seki, M., & Han, K. (eds.) (2003) *Genchika suru chūgoku shinshutsu kigyō [Localization by Japanese Companies in China]*. Tokyo: Shinhyoron.

Simon, H.A. (1976) *Administrative Behavior* (3rd ed.) New York: Macmillan (1st ed., 1945).

Takahashi, N. (2010) *Kyomō no seikashugi: nihongata nenkōsei hukkatsu no susume [Unrealistic Merit System: Revival of Japanese Seniority-Based System]*. Tokyo: Tsukuma Shobō.

Van Maanenm, J., & Barley, S.R. (1984) Occupational Communities: Culture and Control in Organizations. In Staw, B.M. and Cummings, L.L. (eds.), *Research in Organizational Behaviors (Vol. 6)*, pp. 287–365. Greenwich, CT: JAI Press.

Vogel, E. (1979) *Japan as Number One*. Cambridge, MA: Harvard University Press.

Wolf, E.R. (1956) Aspects of Group Relations in a Complex Society: Mexico. *American Anthropologist*, LVII, pp. 1065–1078.

Wolf, E.R. (1958) The Virgin of Guadalupe: A Mexican National Symbol. *Journal of American Folklore*, 71(1), pp. 34–39.

Wong, H.W. (1999) *Japanese Bosses, Chinese Workers: Power and Control in a Hong Kong Megastore*. Richmond, VA: Curzon Press.

Yahagi, T. (2007) *Kouri kokusaika purosesu: Riron to kēsu de kangaeru [Globalization Process of Retailers: Theories and Case Studies]*. Tokyo: Yuhikaku.

Yoshino, M.Y. (1968) *Japan's Managerial System: Tradition and Innovation*. Cambridge: MIT Press.

2 Formation of Corporate Ideology

This chapter examines the formation of its corporate ideology based on the economic background of Ichi[1] in Japan, its development in multiple markets, and the founder's legacy. The Japanese company is an elementary entity pursuing distinctive activities that do not overlap with those of other organizations in its industry, which Rodney Clark claims is characteristic of the Japanese company (1979: 49). I will discuss how this distinctiveness and its particular economic background led the company to change from a regional retailer to a nationwide Japanese company. It is crucial to demonstrate how the company's managerial strategies are largely influenced by the founder's legacy and its overseas expansion

Japanese Apparel Market Overview

In 2012, Japan's real gross domestic product (GDP) was 1.2%, and its nominal GDP was 0.3% based on data provided by the Cabinet Office of the government of Japan. According to the Teikoku Databank, Japan's 2011 economic growth was negative, mainly due to the Great East Japan Earthquake that occurred on March 11, 2011; moreover, the strong yen reduced exports for two years while imports increased because of the poor supply due to the disaster and the need for production recovery (2012). The Teikoku Databank's 2013 data reflect economic policies, such as public investments worth five trillion yen and credit relaxation, designed to spur the domestic economy and that are expected to increase exports and consumption (Teikoku Databank, 2013: 1).

Data in the Final Consumption Expenditure of Households of the Japanese government's Cabinet Office show that national expenditures on apparel products and accessories decreased from 12 trillion yen in 2001 to nine trillion yen in 2011 and that apparel product and accessory expenditures decreased as a percentage of total expenditures from 4.3% in 2001 to 3.43% in 2011. Moreover, while the supply volume increased 2.5 times, the retail value dropped to two-thirds of the previous year's total (Mizuho Corporate Bank, 2012: 1–2).

Before discussing recent trends in Japan's apparel industry, we will draw from Kinoshita (2004) in a brief review of the historical development that

DOI: 10.4324/9781003305675-2

reveals how the industry emerged and how competition shifted from the domestic level to the global one. The years 1951 to 1973 could be regarded as the period of the emergence of the apparel industry in Japan. The word "apparel" (*apareru*) started being used around 1970 to indicate products that had a higher value and fashion sense than "clothing" (*iryōhin*; Kinoshita, 2004: 134, 167). The core element in Japanese apparel had traditionally been the kimono, for which people bought fabrics rather than ready-made clothing. The introduction of ready-to-wear products was supported by the Japanese government during the nation's wartime periods from 1870 to 1923 when military uniforms were urgently needed although the network of nationwide sales channel was limited. From 1951 to 1973, during the energy crisis, ready-made products emerged as a new industry as the nation moved from order-made to ready-made. Before 1960, department stores were more familiar with overseas fashion trends than textile wholesalers, and customers were more attracted by department store brands than by manufacturer brands. However, customers were gradually attracted by the manufacturers, who also began to promote their brands (Kinoshita, 2004: 157).

From 1973 to 1990, manufacturers gradually began to establish a variety of brands, locations, and store strategies. Manufacturers used brands for different locations, such as department stores and supermarkets, to segment their business. During the 1970s, many fashion buildings housing clothing shops appeared; in the early 1980s, these shops introduced discount brands from overseas, and large retailers started to integrate tenants into their shopping malls as Japan's motorization progressed (Kinoshita, 2004: 161).

The period from 1990 to the present has been marked by the emergence of a business model that combines production with retail and fierce competition among both domestic and global retailers. In the 1990s, the bursting of the bubble reduced commodity prices. Retailers were forced to maintain profits, minimize losses, and build their brands, by shifting their business model to the "speciality store retailer of a private label apparel" (SPA) model (Kinoshita, 2004: 163–164). The traditional retail structure of Japanese apparel products had three middle sectors – the first wholesaler, the second wholesaler, and the retailer – between the manufacturers and the customers. The SPA model has the advantage of being a simple retail structure, making products in ways companies expect and providing customers with affordable prices due to the lack of a margin for the middle sectors. To practice SPA, companies needed the power of development, purchasing, selling, and branding. To save on costs, Japanese retailers started to transfer their production sites to China during the 1990s (Mizuho Corporate Bank, 2012: 1). After abolition of the Large-scale Retail Stores Law (*daitenhō*) in 2000, customers were able to buy products at reasonable prices rather than just luxury ones in Japan's large shopping malls (Mizuho Corporate Bank, 2012: 1–2).

The mid-1990s saw not only an increase in imported apparel products from the West and China but also the entry of global fashion giants into the

Japanese market, resulting in fierce competition. The first global fashion retailer entrant was The Gap, which opened in Ginza, Tokyo, in 1995. Later, in 1998, the Spanish brand ZARA entered the market in Shibuya, Tokyo. In 2006, the UK brand TOPSHOP opened in Harajuku, Tokyo. In 2008, the leading fashion company Hennes & Mauritz (H&M) arrived in Japan and opened its first store in Ginza, Tokyo. The Japanese media reported the wide popularity of the Ginza H & M store, and many customers lined up for its opening. In April 2009, another youth-targeted apparel firm, Forever 21, arrived in Harajuku, Tokyo, and attracted many Japanese young people. In April 2012, American Eagle Outfitters opened its first store in Harajuku. While most worldwide fashion retailers started in Tokyo, some chose to open in Osaka or Yokohama. In March 2013, MIXXO, a brand owned by the Korean apparel company ELAND, opened its first store in Yokohama. In June 2013, MONKI and WEEKDAY, H&M brands, opened stores in Ebisubashi, Osaka. Whenever a large foreign apparel company opened its first Japanese store, admission limitations were imposed, forcing customers to wait for more than several hours.

As global fashion retailers began to appear, people started to use the term "fast fashion" to refer to affordable trendy fashion products. These were based on the SPA model, similar to Ichi's, in which the company is responsible for the design, production, and distribution, thus achieving "fastness."[2] The fast fashion phenomenon has several other distinctive features. According to Japanese retail specialist Kotaro Kawashima, fast fashion has three features: low price, high quality, and fashion ability (2009: 14). Cachon and Swinney add that fast fashion companies need to respond to trends quickly and have strong design teams (2011: 778). It has also been argued that fast fashion encourages disposability (Fletcher, 2008), and the sustainability and ethical appeal of fast fashion have been debated (Aspers and Skov, 2006; Emberley, 1998; John et al., 2012).

While establishing their market positions in Japan by borrowing the power of department stores to create their brands, apparel manufacturers also merged production and retail functions after the economic downturn caused by the burst bubble. Although many Japanese customers favored the above trendy fashionable brands, some of them doubted the quality of these brands. In recent years, the basis of the competition felt by apparel companies in Japan has shifted from price to high-value-added products and many Japanese fashion enterprises faced fierce competition from global fashion leaders. To seek potential markets, some Japanese apparel retailers have sought overseas markets; however, the number was limited. A 2012 report by the Japan External Trade Organization showed that, among 2,769 Japanese companies, only 78 retailers were operating overseas.

In this severe competition, a former regional retailer was able to grow very successfully. That is Ichi. In the next section, I will describe how Ichi was able to secure its market position in Japan under such an economic environment and gained high popularity in overseas markets.

From a Regional Retailer to a Nationwide Company

Despite the challenging market environment, Ichi's mother company, Ichi Retailing, was ranked tenth among Japanese retailers and first among apparel companies in the domestic market according to statistics published by the Stores and National Retail Federation in 2012.[3] Moreover, Ichi's founder announced that the company's 2020 goal would be to become the number one apparel firm with $50 billion in revenues.

Given its net sales, Ichi Retailing's presence gradually became apparent in the world market. Ichi Retailing was ranked within the top five SPA companies by the end of 2012 based on Stores and NRF data. Inditex, which owns the ZARA brand, was ranked first followed by H&M. The Gap, avant-courier of SPA and casual wear, was ranked third, and U.S. company Limited Brands was ranked fourth. Fifth-ranked Ichi Retailing was the first Japanese apparel company to rank within the global top five. According to the company's 2012 annual report, its net sales totaled 9,286 billion yen, and it achieved a net income of 716 billion yen. Along with this increase in net sales, the foreign media became interested in the global presence of the company founder, whose overall wealth of $133 billion made him Japan's richest person in 2013. Sakai had this honor in 2009 and 2012. As of April 22 2013, Sakai owns around 45% of Ichi Retailing, making him worth $17 billion (in stock value).

Ichi Retailing comprised three major operations – Ichi Japan, Ichi International, and Global Brands – in August 2012. Ichi Japan, with 845 stores, achieved 66.8% of total net sales, totaling 620 billion yen. Ichi International, comprising all overseas operations, with 292 stores, had net sales of 153 billion yen. Global Brands, comprising one local and three overseas brands and operating 1,085 stores (including franchise stores), had net sales of 153 billion yen.

Ichi continuously increased its net sales and its stores both in Japan and overseas markets between 1992 and 2012 (see Figure 2.1). By August 2012, Ichi operated 1,736 stores worldwide, including 845 in the domestic market and 292 in overseas markets. As the figure shows, its stores multiplied quickly after 2005, primarily overseas and after the mergers and acquisitions (M&A) of domestic and global brands.

The company's net sales increased sharply in 2001 because of the fleece campaign, discussed later, and again in 2011 when another successful Ichi product was released, showing the close relationship between products and net sales. Ichi products have been highly evaluated by customers because of its four core product principles – high-value-added, affordable prices, high quality, and casual wear. Besides their products, Ichi's increased net sales in overseas markets have also contributed to this change.

The above figure illustrates Ichi's current situation, regarded as a "legend" in Japan, and its Asian and global position. The company's operations are inevitably linked to Ichi's historical development and principles. I will discuss

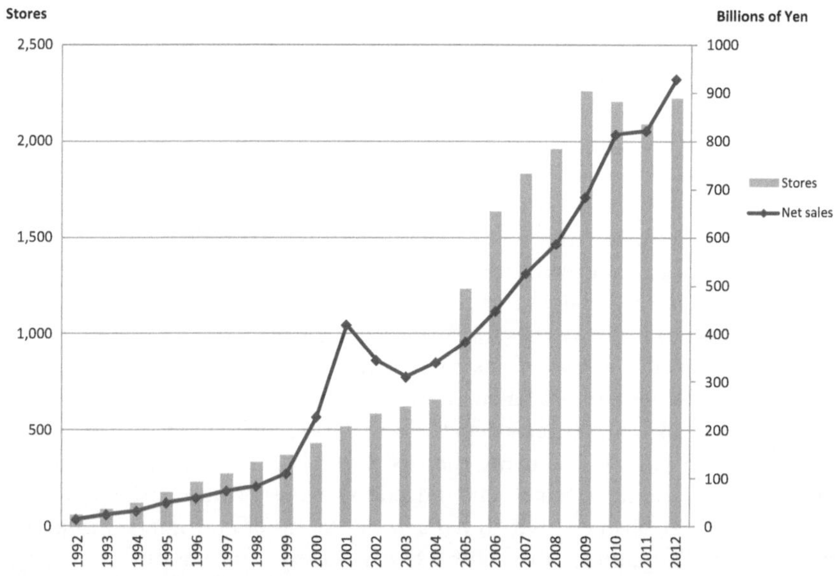

Figure 2.1 Net sales and number of Ichi stores (1992–2012), created by the author.

the biography of the founder, Takahiro Sakai, one of the key influences on the formation of Ichi ideology.

Founder Philosophy and Corporate Ideology

Ichi founder Takahiro Sakai was born in 1949 and lived with his parents and a younger sister in Yamaguchi Prefecture in southwestern Japan before entering university in Tokyo. That same year, Sakai's father opened a men's clothing shop specializing in high-end suits while his father also owned a construction company. Sakai expected his father that he would be able to receive a good education. After graduating from high school, Sakai entered a private university in Japan to study politics and economics. At one point, his studies were interrupted for a year because of the student movement, and he was reluctant to study. Though Sakai had wished to work for a major Japanese *shōsha* (trading firm), he was rejected because no companies were willing to spend time and money on someone likely to be a successor in the family business.

Sakai had been strongly influenced by his father, who had high expectations for him and encouraged him to be the best in his field. Besides spiritual encouragement, Sakai received economic support from his father. Sakai recalled during an interview with a magazine that the most precious aspect of his university life was when his father generously gave him money to travel around the world when he was in his second year.[4] This experience influenced not only Sakai's awareness of globalization but also his way of thinking about business.

When Sakai failed the trading firm qualifying examinations, Sakai's father used his connections to help Sakai join a large Japanese retailer, JUSCO. However, Sakai quit after less than a year because of the gap he perceived between the advanced retail system he had observed overseas and the underdeveloped Japanese model. Afterwards, he moved in with his then-girlfriend, his current wife, in Tokyo and prepared to study overseas although he basically did nothing there. After half a year, Sakai was persuaded by his father to go back to Yamaguchi Prefecture in 1972 and work on the front line while thinking about the company's future.

Sakai wanted to improve the store's poor efficiency. Although many senior employees resigned because of Sakai's reforms, his father did not intervene. One day in 1974, he handed Sakai all of the clothing company's files. In his autobiography, Sakai says that he decided at that moment never to fail the business. He was 25 years old. During the first several years, Sakai pondered the disadvantages of the suit business and started to seriously consider the potential of the casual wear business, which has a wider range of customers. Living in a small city in Yamaguchi Prefecture, Sakai gained information by reading fashion magazines and going overseas every year to observe advanced retailers, especially chain stores, where Sakai started buying clothing and accessories.

Sakai was eager to learn the advanced Western system and hoped to improve his stores' efficiency as much as possible. He was also starting to pay attention to the casual wear market. Sakai's hungry spirit, which was influenced by his father and by his strong curiosity, allowed him to find ideas for future development.

The first idea for Ichi came during Sakai's visit to a U.S. university co-op store. He noticed the store's self-service, full-volume, customer-oriented floor plan, which gave him the idea for Ichi's self-service principle. When major SPA companies, such as the Gap, Limited, and chain stores using self-service business models, began appearing in the 1980s, Sakai discovered a market for low-priced casual wear among young people

To explore this new market, Sakai opened the first Ichi store in Hiroshima in 1984. The entire company was named "Ichi," and Sakai became its president. In 1985, the company opened its first "roadside" store,[5] which became a major location strategy.

Sakai believed that few companies were able to offer affordable high-quality casual wear at that time. To meet this market need, Sakai met the Hong Kong-based founder of Giordano, a fashion retailer with an SPA model. Sakai learned that managing the production site was necessary to ensure high quality. In 1987, the company started to create their products. In 1991, the company changed its name to "Ichi Retailing" and established chain stores. The company opened an average of 30 stores a year; the number of stores increased from 29 to 109 between 1991 and 1994. In 1997, Ichi went public on the Tokyo Stock Exchange.

Ichi established its SPA model gradually. The huge success of its 1998 fleece campaign in Harajuku, the heart of Tokyo, proved that the company's strategy meets customers' needs. Two million pieces of Ichi fleece were sold in the first season, and, by the winter of 1999, more than five and a half million fleece pieces had been sold; by 2000, this number had increased to 26 million. There has been no other large Japanese company that has increased its sales from 100 billion yen to 400 billion within only two years. Four core product principles including high-value-added, affordable prices, high quality and casual wear, played a significant role in such achievement. The founder particularly focused on two principles – high-value-added and high quality – so he collaborated with other Japanese companies to create innovative products and sent specialists to factories to make sure the quality been maintained. The founder believed that these two core principles distinguish Ichi from other retailers who also sell casual wear at affordable prices.

By 2000, Ichi had covered all of Japan's cities and prefectures. Since the beginning of Ichi and Ichi Retailing, Sakai had worked as chairman (*kaichō*) and president (*shachō*). In 2002, Sakai handed the presidency over to an employee who had been recruited mid-career in 1998. Sakai then became chairman of the group. Although net sales increased in 2004, the company increased its net sales and suffered reduced profits without making any investments or pursuing M&A. Sakai was worried, since he believed that this indicated inefficiency; he was also dissatisfied with the company's management style, which valued stability. During his return as the CEO of Ichi, he announced an agenda that included the globalization of the company's market, production, operations, human resources, management, and other operational components.

Gradually and successfully Ichi, a regional fashion retailer, changed into a nationwide retailer on an SPA model during the economic downturn by pursuing a high job efficiency level and by "creating customers" using four key concepts: high-value-added, affordable prices, high-quality, and casual wear. Creating customers was a major mission for the company according to writer and consultant Peter Drucker. Sakai, who admires Drucker, has commented that this idea encouraged him to move forward and create new products.

Besides product strategy, another founder's philosophy is globalization with the goal of becoming become number one apparel company in the world. To increase sales and secure its market position, Ichi's overseas stores increased continuously, and its overseas sales improved; however, its overseas expansion initially suffered many failures. The company established a subsidiary in June 2000 in the U.K., which opened its first store in 2001. In 2002, the company opened a store in Shanghai, China, its second market. However, overseas operations did not go well initially. The company closed many of its 23 U.K. stores in 2003, leaving only five open. The situation in China was not ideal, and the company had to close all its Beijing stores in 2005. Sakai concluded that the major reason for the failure in the U.K. was the over-localized human personnel and the rapid opening of new stores before brand visibility had been achieved. Sakai also claimed that the localization of products was the major cause of the failure in mainland China.

In 2005, the company entered the Hong Kong market and enjoyed huge sales and popularity, which Sakai believed was due to the application of Ichi Japan's system, which he called the "Ichi DNA." The failures in the U.K. and mainland China prompted Sakai to emphasize the standardization of this Ichi DNA over localization. Another major breakthrough in the overseas market was helped by the opening of flagship stores, designed to enhance the brand image. Ichi started to build its brand by opening flagship stores, starting in Soho, New York City, in 2006; this store paid high rent and attracted much local and global media attention. Ichi opened flagship stores in London (2007), Paris (2009), and Shanghai (2010). By early 2013, the company had opened four global flagship stores, including one in Taipei, Taiwan, one on Fifth Avenue, New York, Seoul, Korea, and one in Hong Kong.

The number of Ichi stores in overseas markets shows that the company's strategy has been focused more on overseas operations. By August 2012, the business of Ichi International had expanded into 12 countries, eight in Asia and the others in the U.S., the U.K., France, and Russia (see Table 2.1). By the end of 2012, Ichi had opened 25 stores in Japan and closed 23 existing stores. The total number of Japanese stores has changed little. Ichi International has opened 115 stores and closed four.

In addition to the growth in stores, net sales have also been strong. The net sales of Ichi Japan increased by 3.3% in 2011, with the company reducing its operating income by 3.6%. Unlike in Japan, the net sales of Ichi International increased by 63.4% and its operating income increased by 22.9%.

Table 2.1 Numbers of Ichi stores, 2012

Country or Region	*Total*	*Opened*	*Closed*
Ichi Japan	845	25	23
Directly-operated	824	24	22
Franchise	21	1	1
Ichi International	292	115	4
China	145	65	0
Hong Kong	16	1	0
Taiwan	17	16	0
South Korea	80	18	0
Singapore	7	2	0
Malaysia	5	3	0
Thailand	4	4	0
Philippines	1	1	0
U.K.	10	2	3
U.S.	3	2	0
France	2	1	0
Russia	2	0	1

Created by the author.

The company founder began to emphasize the necessity of a globalized system and a unique brand image for the company. The major principle of Ichi's globalization policy was illustrated by the "Global One" concept, the attempt to standardize operations throughout Ichi stores all over the world. Sakai claimed that this policy aimed to encourage the company to become unified and develop the best practices in the world. The Operations Manager of the Hong Kong subsidiary added that, as the distinctive feature of Ichi was the SPA model, which required every store to sell particular products within certain periods of time, standardization was crucial to Ichi operations in all markets. The company intended to preserve its DNA and it is a "new type" of Japanese company.

To establish and maintain standardization of Ichi DNA, the company sent expatriates who were supposed to possess the company's DNA and decentralized authority, delegating to the local Store Managers, who were expected to contribute to profit-making by promoting standardization, making decisions quickly, and improving the company.

One of the major mediators of standardization was the relocation of experienced Japanese expatriates to overseas markets. Ichi's 2010 agenda, the *minzoku daiidō* (ethnic movement), is a representative example. Sakai's corporate report describes this as the process of establishing strong stores and a global headquarters, opening large stores, and relocating Research and Development (R&D). The company has announced the relocation of approximately 800 Japanese Store Managers and 100 Japanese managers to overseas stores for at least three years. To unify its stores, the company plans to educate candidates in Japan before new stores open. The company has also announced that it has already moved around 150 employees from the production and R&D departments to Shanghai, China, to improve quality and enhance stock control.

The company delegated authority to the Store Managers, who were then expected to contribute to the company's standardization, fast decision-making, and store improvements. Standardization was necessary at the stores and the profit-making centers and Store Managers were responsible for introducing the standardized requirements, called *kijun* (standard), which were intended to enhance cost performance. One of the principles of Ichi Retailing's approach to add value is speed, which allows a company to adapt to changes immediately and secure a strong market position. The company stresses the crucial role of communication from the *genba* (front line) to the office. To allow front-line employees to make suggestions, the company introduced a system that, addressing the company's human resources and hierarchy, is designed to prompt Store Managers to create a company that focuses on its stores rather than on adherence to the top-down model. Moreover, Sakai stresses that the store manager should become the major players in the company and that their salaries should depend on their skills rather than on their seniority. Sakai emphasizes that, while store employees will still seek to become Store Managers (given their higher salaries and the possibility of fast promotion), the Head Office will be responsible for educating specialists.

Store managers are also expected to motivate employees to participate in management, reflecting the *zen'in keiei* idea proposed by Konosuke Matsushita, the founder of Panasonic, which asserts that employees must see themselves as self-employed individuals able to manage the stores themselves rather than merely following their superiors and that a company must manage crises. As *zen'in keiei* requires individual participation, Sakai stresses that companies must transfer a certain degree of authority to each individual, especially to front-line workers, rather than allowing the system to manage every employee.

In addition to the practical and rational considerations, Ichi also enhanced its software strategy of building a "Japanese-like" brand image, regarded as a necessary strategy for Japanese retailers in overseas markets (Sakaguchi, 2010; Shimada, 2011). A distinctive feature of Ichi's strategy was that it introduced the practice of Ichi-specific customer satisfaction (CS) to its overseas stores by making it a standard requirement; employees were expected to achieve higher CS and help the company build a unique brand image.

The above description explains how Ichi ideology has been formed based on the founder's legacy, and failures in the U.K. and mainland China. Ichi's ideology is distinct in the sense that it emphasizes the standardization of its DNA rather than localization.

Conclusion

This chapter has examined Japan's apparel market to understand the background of Ichi's emergence and transformation from a regional retailer to a nationwide company based on its unique business strategy. I have investigated the fundamental elements of the management principles underlying Ichi ideology and its influence on the company's overseas expansion strategy and globalization policy.

Ichi emerged during the recession and succeeded because it created new groups of customers based on its SPA model combining four key concepts – high value-added, reasonable prices, high quality, and casual wear – while many other companies competed on the bases of low prices and trends. A corporate ideology closely linked to the founder's management philosophy has strongly influenced Ichi's managerial practices. Founder Takahiro Sakai pursued quick turnover and worked strenuously against the urge to rely on safe, steady, and slow growth.

Faced with a shrinking national market and the entry of global fashion leaders, Ichi sought opportunities overseas, a strategy promoted by Sakai, who has repeatedly emphasized the role of global markets in the quick pace of development. Overseas expansion did not begin smoothly, but success in Hong Kong convinced the company to standardize its Ichi DNA, including its job efficiency, CS, and the decentralization of power in favor of the Store Managers in the local markets rather than adapting to the local situation. The Ichi DNA, reflecting its corporate ideology, is a core part of the company's globalization strategy, the "Global One" policy, which aimed to standardize the company's operations based on the standardized ideology applied abroad.

In the next chapter, I examine the significant marketing factors that contributed to the company's success in Hong Kong and Ichi's gradual introduction of its DNA and standardized system under the "Global One" policy. I then move on to the company's operations by examining its Hong Kong subsidiary's organizational structure, particularly its Ichi stores, which are the fundamental components of the company.

Notes

1 To avoid revealing the identity of the company, I refrain from citing the source related to Ichi in this book.
2 This term was first used by a speaker at the 1987 GAP stockholders' meeting. A Japanese reporter shortened it to "SPA," the Japanese translation of *seizō kourigyō* (manufacturing retailer), because companies do not only manufacture but also distribute their products (*Senken shinbunsha* 1999: 4–5).
3 The top ten Japanese retailers included one electronics retailer (Yamada Denki), five supermarket, hypermarket, and related businesses (AEON, Seven & i Holdings, UNY, The Daiei, Beisia Group), and three department stores (Isetan Mitsukoshi Holdings, J. Front Retailing, and Takashimaya).
4 Sakai's father gave him two million yen, the equivalent of around 1–200 million yen today.
5 The term "roadside" means that the store is located near a busy road to attract customers. Most such stores are located outside the cities.

References

Aspers, P., & Lise, S. (2006) Encounters in the Global Fashion Business. *Current Sociology*, 54, pp. 745–763.

Cachon, G.P., & Swinney, R. (2011) The Value of Fast Fashion: Quick Response, Enhanced Design, and Strategic Consumer Behavior. *Management Science*, 57(4), pp. 778–795.

Clark, R. (1979) *The Japanese Company*. Cambridge, MA: Yale University Press.

Clark, R. (2013) *nendo no gyōseki mitōshi ni kansuru kigyō no ishiki chōsa.* [*Research on the Company's Prospects towards the Business Practice in 2013*] Teikoku Databank. Available at: https://www.tdb-di.com/special-planning-survey/sp20130411.php.

Emberley, J.V. (1998) *Venus and Furs: The Cultural Politics of Fur.* London: I.B. Tauris & Co.

Fletcher, K. (2008) *Sustainable Fashion & Textiles: Design Journeys.* Oxford: Earthscan.

Joy, A, Sherry, J.F, Venkatesh, A, Wang, J., & Chan, R. (2012) Fast Fashion, Sustainability, and the Ethical Appeal of Luxury Brands. *Fashion Theory,* 16(3), pp. 273–296.

Kawashima, K. (2009) *Fasuto fasshon sensou.* Tokyo: Sankeishinbun shuppan.

Kinoshita, A. (2004) Iryōhin ryūtsū –Komodhithi kara burando heno tankan. [Apparel retail: Transformation from commodity to brand] In Ishihara, Takemasa; Yahagi, Toshiyuki (eds.), *Nihon no ryūtsū 100 nen.* [*Japanese 100-Year Distribution: Marketing Channels, Retailing and Public Policy Issues*], pp. 133–174. Tokyo: Yuhikaku.

Mizuho Corporate Bank. (2012) *Mizuho Short Industry Focus: nihon apareru kigyō no kaigaishinshutsu to gurōbaru burando heno shinka.* [*Overseas Expansion and Global Branding by Japanese Apparel Companies*]. Mizuho Corporate Bank. PDF file.

Sakaguchi, M. (2010) Seichō senryaku naki apareru kigyō ha tōta sareru [Apparel Companies without Development Strategy Will Lose Market] *Sn'i torendo [Trends in fiber].* Nov & Dec, pp. 26–30. Available at https://cs2.toray.co.jp/news/tbr/newsrrs01.nsf/0/7995828D5385233B49258353001646C5/$FILE/tre_a117.pdf

Senken shinbunsha. (1999) *Nihonryū SPA no chōsen: fasshon bijinesu seichō no jyōken.* [*Japanese Way of Challenging SPA: Premises for Development of Fashion Business*] Tokyo: Senken shinbunsha.

Shimada, M. (2011) Toyota tsūshō no kaigai fasshon ritēru bijinesu [Fashion Retail Business of Toyota Tsusho]. *JTC Monthly.* February 2011, pp. 18–20.

3 Reframing Ichi Ideology in Hong Kong

The previous chapter examined how Japan's market environment and Ichi's business strategies allowed the company to achieve high domestic popularity and how the company's corporate ideology has been formed. In this chapter, I will examine how Ichi succeeded in Hong Kong locally and then gradually introduced and stressed its corporate ideology under the policy name "Global One" policy. I will then move to the examination of the fundamental components of Ichi: the head office and the store. I will discuss the organizational structure of the stores and local head offices to describe the stores' different degrees of decentralized power or, more precisely, that of the Store Managers. For this detailed examination of store structures, I use the case of the East Point City (EPC) store.

Economic Background of Hong Kong

I will describe the emergence and development of the major pull factor of the Hong Kong retail market, which has become a new travel destination for mainland Chinese tourists. I will also describe the severe rent problem apparel retailers had to face while competing in the market.

On 1 July 1997, Hong Kong's sovereignty was returned to China. The International Monetary Fund (IMF) has described Hong Kong's post-handover economy as having an increasing income inequality and property markets requiring policies that address the macroeconomic and financial risks in the housing market (IMF, 2012). Moreover, as a small and highly open economy, Hong Kong is exposed to global shocks and is relatively volatile (IMF, 2012). Let us briefly examine Hong Kong's recovery from the recession.

After the handover, Hong Kong experienced three external shocks (Martin, 2007). The first external shock was the Asian Financial Crisis which began in 1997 after two rounds of currency depreciation (Nanto, 1998). During the second round, the Hong Kong dollar (among others) was hit. In the third quarter of 1998, property prices in Hong Kong fell nearly 40%. The second external shock was the bursting of the so-called "dot.com" bubble, which led to losses on the Hong Kong Stock Exchange in 2000. The September 11, 2001, attack on the World Trade Center in New York has been regarded as a possible cause

DOI: 10.4324/9781003305675-3

of the decline in Hong Kong tourism (Martin, 2007: 20). The third shock was the Severe Acute Respiratory Syndrome (SARS) epidemic lasting from November 2002 to July 2003, when 299 Hong Kong residents died. Martin explains that SARS had two sets of impacts on Hong Kong's economy – reduced tourism and a decline in the local retail business (Martin, 2007: 20). According to Martin, the recovery of Hong Kong's economy slowed when Tung, the Chief Executive, focused on promoting Hong Kong's basic law Article 23 proposals rather than facilitating Hong Kong's economic recovery (2007: 20).

Based on Hong Kong's Census and Statistics Department (CSD) statistics, Hong Kong's real GDP growth dropped by 5.5% in 1998, recovering the next year at 4.0% and in 2000 with 10.0%. However, after another set of external shocks, it dropped again in 2001 to 0.6% and then grew to 3.2% in 2003. Because of the serious economic losses caused by those external shocks, companies in Hong Kong have reduced their investment flows while China's economy has rapidly grown. The 2003 free trade agreement, the Closer Economic Partnership Arrangement, which includes the new Individual Visit Scheme (IVS) travel policy, plays significant roles in Hong Kong industries, including the clothing industry.

An increase in mainland Chinese tourism has been observed, especially after the IVS was passed. In 2003, the scheme covered ten cities and provinces; in 2004, more than 15 cities were added, along with all the cities in Guangdong, China (in May). In 2003, mainland visitors totaled 2.4 million; in 2004, this increased to 12.25 million. The percentage of IVS visitors out of the total number of mainland visitors to Hong Kong increased from 5.2% in 2003 to 34.8% in 2004. Nearly 70% of all tourists to the city were mainland Chinese in 2011, and they spent an average of 30% more than those from other countries (Yu, 2012).

According to Fan and Yim, the number of mainland Chinese visitors out of the total number of visitors increased from 18.4% in 1996 to 63.0% in 2010 (2011: 4). They add that tourism is the fastest-growing of Hong Kong's Four Pillar Industries and that the mainland factor is increasingly important to growth (2011: 9).[1] The Hong Kong Tourism Board indicates that visitors to Hong Kong totaled 427 million by the end of April 2013, an increase of 11.5% over the previous year. Mainland Chinese constituted the highest growth rate, 17.5%; 311 million visited Hong Kong by April 2013.

A research paper produced by the Hang Seng bank describes the importance of mainland Chinese tourists to Hong Kong tourism since they are big spenders (Fan and Yim, 2011: 1). In 2010, each mainland visitor spent HK$7,453 in Hong Kong. This tourist spending consists mainly of shopping rather than staying in luxury hotels (Fan and Yim. 2011: 5–6). Many visitors who did not stay overnight spent the most, around HK$2,356 (Fan and Yim, 2011: 4). Jones Lang LaSalle has commented that "Hong Kong will continue to enjoy a 10 to 15% growth in Chinese visitor arrivals per year" (Yu, 2012).

As IVS coverage increases, the impact of mainland Chinese visitors on retail, including the clothing industry, cannot be underestimated. During the

PRC's 2012 National Day Golden Week, the number of mainland Chinese tourists increased to 41,000, 6% over the previous month (Ruo, 2012). The average spending by mainland Chinese in Hong Kong is around HK$12,000, and clothing is the third most popular item, representing 45% of planned purchase lists ("Mainland Tourists Tripling," 2011).

According to 2011 data, more shops were opened by international retailers in Hong Kong than anywhere else in the Asia-Pacific region (Leung, 2013), indicating the popularity of Hong Kong's market. Global fashion giants following the speciality store retailer of a private label apparel model such as H&M, ZARA, GAP, Abercrombie&Fitch, and Forever 21 have all entered the Hong Kong market, as have Japanese apparel retailers such as point, WORLD, Liz Lisa, and Onward Kashiyama, attracted mainly by the softening in retail spaces.

The popularity of the Hong Kong market was represented by the increase in its retail rent particularly in the shopping district. One of Hong Kong's major shopping areas, Causeway Bay, has rents that exceed those on New York's Fifth Avenue ("Hong Kong's Causeway Bay", 2012). Its rent per square is now $2,630, compared to $2,500 in New York and $1,129 on the Champs-Elysees in Paris. The rents in the city's central district have also grown by 21.8%. However, global retailers do not hesitate to pay expensive rent. For instance, Abercrombie&Fitch, which opened a flagship store in the city's central area in August 2012, paid $1 million per month, and Forever 21, which opened a store near Causeway Bay in January 2012, paid $1.4 million a month for a lease, almost as much rent paid by ZARA; H&M paid more than double that price for its large-scale store in the central area ("ChinaDaily," 2012).

I have discussed how the new IVS travel policy and the increase in its coverage produced a large flow of rich mainland Chinese tourists, who helped expand the apparel market. While many global and Japanese apparel retailers have entered the market to enjoy the increase in Hong Kong's cash flows, they have also suffered from expensive rent prices. In the following section, I will discuss how Ichi, under severe competition, was able to position itself strongly and gain wide popularity.

Ichi's Development in Hong Kong

On April 26, 2013, at the opening of the flagship store, Sakai stated that the Hong Kong market played a significant role in Ichi's overseas operations because the Hong Kong store was the first to operate in the black from the very beginning, while other overseas stores were still in the red. When Ichi entered the Hong Kong market in 2005, the company's annual report evaluated the market as being the "model for Ichi's entry into overseas markets." The market produced one billion yen in net income in the first fiscal year. Remarkably, the operational profits from the Hong Kong market were ranked first among all overseas markets for several years even though rents and labor costs were high.

By June 2013, there were 17 stores in Hong Kong (see Table 3.1; the number of stores is calculated according to fiscal year, from August to September of the following year). The first store in Hong Kong, Miramar, opened in September 2005. In the 2007 fiscal year, three stores opened, and four more opened in the 2008 fiscal year. By the end of August 2007, the company had earned HK$1.8 billion, including operating profits of HK$46 million. The number of new stores dropped from four to two, with the peak in the fiscal year 2008. In the fiscal year 2011, the company started to convert its standardized stores into large-scale ones,[2] such as the Telford Plaza store and the Harbor City store.

As to location strategy, only four out of the 17 stores were located in major shopping areas, such as the Miramar store in Tsim Sha Tsui and the Lee Theatre store in Causeway Bay, to limit rental costs. Others were located in residential areas, and some were intended to attract mainland Chinese tourists, such as the New Town Plaza store in Shatin, the Maritime Square store in Tsing Yi, and the store in Tuen Mun. These locations are easier for mainland Chinese tourists to access: they can reach Shatin via the East Rail Line, which directly connects to the station in Shenzhen on the mainland; others can visit the Tsing Yi store on their way to or from Hong Kong's international airport. There are also 24 hour direct bus services from the station to mainland China near the Telford Plaza store. Therefore, we can assume that the company's location strategy tends to target not only local residents but also mainland Chinese tourists.

An overview of Ichi's Hong Kong operations gave an impression of the company's relatively stable store and sales development. A detailed examination

Table 3.1 Number and location of Ichi stores, 2005–2013

Opening year	*Number of stores*	*Name of store*	*District*
2005.09–2006.08	1	Miramar	Retail
2006.09–2007.08	2	City Plaza	Business
	3	Festival Walk	Residential
	4	Telford Plaza	Residential
2007.09–2008.08	5	Lee Theatre	Retail
	6	East Point City	Residential
	7	New Town Plaza	Residential
	8	Citywalk	Residential
2008.09–2009.08	9	Plaza Hollywood	Residential
	10	Maritime Square	Residential
	11	World Trade Center	Retail
2009.09–2010.08	12	Harbour City	Retail
	13	tmtplaza	Residential
2010.09–2011.08	Relocation	Telford Plaza	Residential
	14	Olympian City	Residential
	15	Taipo Mega Mall	Residential
2011.09–2012.08	16	apm	Residential
2012.09–2013.08	Relocation	Harbour City	Retail
	Flagship store	Lee Theatre Flagship	Retail
	17	The Edge	Residential

Based on each fiscal year.

will be made of the local subsidiary's development from 2005 onwards and an illustration of the factors that have driven local subsidiaries to such practice by analyzing how the company gradually enhanced the importance of its corporate ideology, Ichi's DNA.

Laissez-Faire Principle: 2005–2007

The chief executive officer (CEO) of Ichi Hong Kong, Zhang Peng, contributed significantly to the sales of the first store in Hong Kong, which opened in the Miramar Shopping Mall, Tsim Sha Tsui, in September 2005. The average monthly sales of the Miramar store hit HK$8 million in the first year, regarded as a huge overseas success. The "legend" of Zhang Peng became famous among Ichi employees. Zhang was born in mainland China and went to university in Japan. After graduating with a master's degree from a private university in Tokyo, Zhang started working at Ichi in 1995. Zhang was promoted to store manager within half a year and was responsible for establishing the business office for production management in Guangzhou, China in 1999. He was appointed CEO of Ichi Hong Kong in March 2005.

Before the opening of the first Ichi store, many Japanese executives doubted the location selection and price strategy proposed by Zhang. He showed footage he had taken near Miramar Shopping Mall and explained that the mall had low rent and was an appropriate location, though many executives claimed that few people were walking in the street and that the shopping mall did not seem popular. Zhang insisted on using Japanese tags and product bags to promote a "Made in Japan" image. Sakai says that this tactic differed from that of the former head of Chinese operations, who proposed selling lower-priced products of lower quality. Zhang believed that the positive image of Japan held by Hong Kong residents could lead to higher revenues because he saw with his own eyes that Hong Kong and Taiwan tourists were the largest tourist groups to patronize Ichi stores when he worked in Japan. Although there are no official statistics, many Hong Kong tourists indeed bought Ichi products as souvenirs for their friends and relatives before Ichi entered the market. Just by Zhang's expectation, the first store became an unexpectedly huge success in 2005. Zhang recalls that the store was full and that customers lined up from the first to the third floor before the opening.

The major factor in Ichi's early success was the market situation, such as the location strategy, and the company's brand building in an attempt to attract customers with a "Made in Japan" image. After the success of the first store, the local subsidiary opened seven new stores in fiscal years 2007 and 2008. The company's location strategy was to target more mainland Chinese tourists. For instance, the metro station near the Festival Walk store, in Kowloon Tong, is on the East Rail Line, which connects directly to mainland China.

Because of the emphasis on increasing the number of store openings, necessary adjustments to human resource policies and management principles were neglected, and the company did not have enough time to introduce much of the "Global One" standardization, which is why I describe this phase as "laissez-faire." Local and Japanese Store Managers were also busy managing store operations and recruiting new employees to keep up with the high turnover rate. An interview with Mizuno, an Operations Manager who relocated to Hong Kong in 2008, can help us understand the situation:

> I am not judging the Japanese person in charge who worked in Hong Kong before my assignment, but there was no system at that time. There were so many customers every day that employees could only care about replenishment without any standardized rules or systems. Moreover, there was no systematic evaluation system, so the resignation rate was serious. The first store in Hong Kong gained huge success, so the subsidiary was expected to open more stores. When I arrived here, I found that it was completely "uncontrolled" (*nobanashi*). When I went to the store, I found no sign of Ichi's basic principles. The Japanese person in charge looked so tired that he looked like he was dying.

Thus, the local employees experienced an "uncontrolled" situation. One full-timer who worked at the EPC store from its opening in 2007 said, "We didn't have any 'Ichi' rules before. We just learned the skills that are required to operate the store. I've heard that our company has some kind of principles, but we don't have to memorize or chorus them." A part-timer at the EPC store agreed with the full-timer by saying that she liked working in Ichi when there were no "silly" rules.

Ichi Hong Kong was able to succeed for reasons similar to those that apply to Japan – the creation of new customers and a proper location strategy – although we cannot neglect the cultural factor in its success. Because of the laissez-faire policy and the lack of Ichi DNA, store operations in the local market varied and differed from each other. Such differences were reinforced by the decentralization of power in favor of Store Managers.

Implementation of the Ichi DNA and the "Global One" Policy: 2008–2010

The laissez-faire policy did not last for a long time. In 2008, the Ichi DNA was introduced to increase profits and unify brand image to an Ichi *kijun* (standard) while also standardizing floor layout and customer service (CS). The Hong Kong subsidiary's first major change was the introduction and standardization of the Ichi DNA, focusing on *kijun* and CS under the "Global One" policy. Mizuno stressed the necessity of using the DNA to differentiate Ichi from others by referring to the company's failure in the U.K.:

> The major reason for Ichi's failure in U.K. was the complete localization. The company recruited local employees as top management and practiced in local ways. However, it didn't work out well. We failed to

> send the message about the goodness of Japanese companies, and what we could offer as a Japanese organization. At the time, customers only regarded us as an Asian company that sold affordable products. In the beginning, some customers might have been interested in our company, but we failed to differentiate ourselves. Then, we introduced them to our strengths, what we achieved as a Japanese company, and the fundamental principles that led to our success. Those are the major reasons for our success in Hong Kong and Korea. The price of the products actually does not matter that much nowadays, since many companies are doing the same thing. We need to show our high value through our attitudes towards work and display the company's DNA to customers; otherwise, we will not differentiate our company from others.

Additional shop floor standards for employees to follow were added to the company's manuals. Through "Global One", many new standards were introduced to the Hong Kong stores on issues such as price pop locations, store layout, and the order of products to provide a unified shop floor to customers. A standardized CS Check Sheet was formulated, and employees were evaluated daily by their higher-ranked employees on their politeness and hospitality; CS became a more important factor in promotions. The introduction of these requirements also became part of the standardization of the "Global One" policy.

The second change was from "showcase" stores to high-volume sales stores. Although the Hong Kong store is much smaller than the Japanese ones, they all sell the same number of products. According to Mizuno, when Ichi arrived in Hong Kong, the sales floor was designed to build a brand image that attracted customers. To do this, the store set aside a large space near the entrance for many mannequins. Mizuno strongly favored this strategy. However, he believed that, as the Ichi brand was now recognized by many Hong Kong customers, it might be time to create a sales floor geared more toward customer satisfaction, as customers had started to complain about the lack of different sizes and colors. To do this, Mizuno believed it necessary to place more products within the limited space. At the end of 2009, Mizuno felt that the sales floor needed to be changed. Mizuno asked a Japanese Visual Merchandising Display (VMD) team to come to Hong Kong, renew the floor plan, and install larger product shelves for the 2010 autumn-winter peak season. For instance, the EPC store had only small product shelves. Starting in mid-2010, Mizuno regularly visited the store with the Supervisor; in September 2010, a number of large tall product shelves were delivered to the store and these were able to contain more products. With larger product shelves, the store's inventory sharply increased.

This change intends to increase sales since its development was slower than in the early days. Ichi believed that a systemic rationalization was necessary to reduce costs as much as possible, which meant that the stores' major task was to reduce costs and increase sales based on the standardized policy rather than implementing local solutions. For instance, Ichi followed the part-timer-focused model in Japan to assign employees flexibly and reduce costs. Although this model was not workable and many Store Managers suggested changing this policy, it has not been changed for more than five years.

The above practice might not directly contribute to the increase in sales in Hong Kong; however, the company continuously stressed the implementation of its DNA.

Enhancement of DNA in the Mature Stage: 2011–

As the company never stopped expecting higher profit, a breakthrough after re-opening stores as larger ones and opening the flagship store turned out to be necessary. The transfer of Japanese Store Managers was also expected to increase sales, given their deep knowledge of the Ichi DNA, which had contributed strongly to sales in Japan. Around the same time, the company attempted to introduce a monthly CS checkup to enhance Ichi's brand image.

The changes in-store formats and the transfer of Japanese expatriates were expected to help stimulate revenue. Two standard-sized stores, the Harbor City and Telford Plaza stores, were relocated and re-opened as larger stores. The Telford Plaza store was the largest in Hong Kong when it opened. Mizuno said that enlarging the store would have been an efficient way of increasing its net revenue, but that its limited retail space and high rent prevented this. Another breakthrough was made in Hong Kong with the flagship store. Before the store opened, Mizuno "predicted" in an interview that it would be necessary to promote the presence of Ichi again:

> I think a breakthrough is crucial for the Hong Kong operation in the near future. There are large apparel retailers, such as H&M, ZARA and GAP, in Hong Kong. Moreover, the Hong Kong market has already matured, and customers have higher requirements. I am sure Ichi has a position in the market, but we need to have another breakthrough in order to win against those leading apparel retailers. A flagship could have that impact and allow Hong Kong's people to see the potential of Ichi. We are going to open such a store in the near future.[3]
>
> It is not possible to maintain annual sales since Ichi employees regard mere maintenance as a backward move. Therefore, we must exceed the annual sales of the previous year. Even though we are entering the mature stage, we have to brush up on our operations.[4]

Besides securing annual sales growth, the company did not neglect to implement its corporate ideology in Hong Kong. The Ichi DNA was enhanced in Hong Kong through the transfer of seven Japanese Store Managers in early 2011, who were assigned to train local Store Managers based on the "original" Ichi DNA to achieve higher cost performance and profits. Most had long experience working at Ichi. Before their arrival, all Japanese employees were ranked above the Store Managers, increasing the number of Japanese expatriates from three to ten. While working next to them, the Japanese Store Managers were expected to provide detailed training.

One of the strategies to unify Ichi's brand image was the April 2011 introduction of the CS Checkup, performed by a mystery shopper from mainland China. This practice was introduced into the Hong Kong market because of its effectiveness in improving CS in mainland China. According to an informant who worked in mainland China, CS in Hong Kong was not checked until 2010, when Japanese top managers were shocked at its low level.

The above practices were attempts to enhance sales and build Ichi's brand image. The changes to the store's format and the enhancements to Ichi's DNA were consequences of the low sales of Hong Kong stores, which the company believed were caused by a lack of Ichi DNA; they believed it crucial to introduce a system that was more efficient. Japanese Store Managers were sent to Hong Kong to enhance the Ichi DNA through their daily supervision of the stores, while CS checkups were used to improve CS and unify the company image.

To understand how these changes were practiced at the store level, I will first analyze the basic components of the local subsidiary: the head office and the stores.

Organizational Structure

No matter how strongly the company expected to enhance its DNA, it is the store that would carry it out. Here I will observe how the store's structure allowed flexibility despite the centralized authority of the store manager by examining the formal internal structure of the EPC store and the informal store ranking, and how the informal store ranking determined the store's degree of autonomy and influenced employees' careers.

Store Structure

At the EPC store, an "Organizational Store Chart" is hung on the wall of the staff room (see Figure 3.1). Though the chart is called an "organizational chart," it shows the store's work tasks rather than its hierarchy, and it usually changes when the store manager is relocated. From March 2011 to August 2011, there were nine full-timers at the store: the store manager, who was the general commander of the store, one Management Trainee, four Advanced Salespersons, and three Full-time Salespersons. There were about 30–40 part-timers.

Work at the store can be divided into two types: managerial work and front-line work. Managerial work was assigned to full-time workers; the tasks included human resources issues, training, inventory control (i.e., men's, women's, and kids'), pops and stickers, and CS. Two to four members were assigned to each task. Front-line work fell into six different categories: cash register, fitting room, alteration, shop floor, back room, and VMD. These tasks were assigned to both full-timers and part-timers. While full-timers

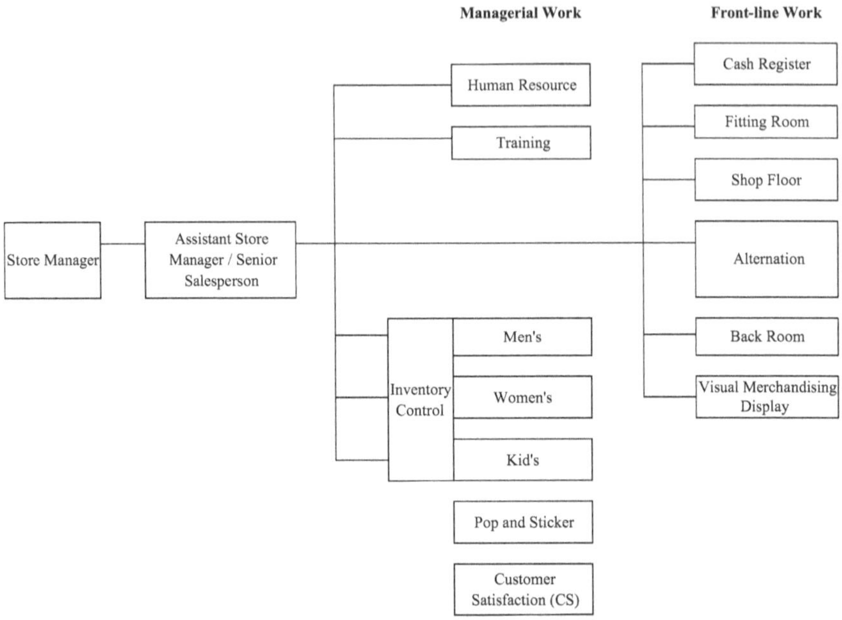

Figure 3.1 Store structure, Ichi, Hong Kong, the EPC store, 2011, created by the author.

shared more than one managerial task, there was no formal division of labor for front-line work, which meant that any staff member could be assigned to do this work.

The division of labor at the store thus overlapped, which I will further discuss in Chapter 5, and only the major characteristics of the structure are examined here. This non-organizational-chart structure at the store reflected the company's belief in the importance of organizational flexibility. Each work task was structured horizontally rather than vertically. Such a horizontal structure enhanced communication among colleagues and fostered information sharing (Aoki, 1986: 972). As they shared the same Ichi knowledge, employees were expected to become multifunctional workers rather than specialists in a specific skill. This reflects what Aoki calls a "horizontal" structure (Aoki, 1986, 1990, 1992). Aoki differentiates between Japanese and Western organizations by stressing that, in Japanese organizations' *J-mode*, as Aoki calls it, coordination is horizontal among operating units, and knowledge is shared among workers rather than retained by individuals with specific skills. The *H-mode*, which represents the Western model, is characterized by the hierarchical separation between planning and on-site operations and by an emphasis on specialization (Aoki, 1990: 8). A flat structure allows worker ownership and a feeling of being influential on corporate management decisions (Aoki, 1990: 23).

Relations between the store manager and other employees were vertical. As the figure shows, subordinates had no obvious hierarchical differentiation among them, but the store manager had the authority to make the final decision. This design was intended to transfer enough authority to the Store Managers to motivate them to play their role as a "manager" (*keieisha*) of the company, so the founder claims, and offer valuable information to the company's operations. This centralized authority allowed us to observe the dependence of the employees on the Store Managers, which I will focus on in Chapter 7.

Informal store rankings largely decided the status and autonomy of each Hong Kong store and the career paths of the employees. According to a local store manager, the idea for this informal ranking was presented by Operations Manager Mizuno as a way of assigning Store Managers. This was an informal method since the company had claimed that each store should be treated equally. When I questioned this informal ranking the Japanese store manager, he answered,

> I believe that the leader and other executives would say that your understanding is not correct. But, honestly, it is hard to comment on that. I understand your claim, but our company specializes in standardization and simplification. So I am quite sure that top higher ranked employees basically would not admit that there is difference of importance between large size stores and smaller stores.

My fieldwork data show that the stores were divided into three basic categories: A-rank, B+-rank, and B-rank (see Table 3.2). This list is a general

Table 3.2 Informal ranking of stores, Hong Kong, 2011

Rank	*Stores*	*Location*	*Areas*
A	Miramar	Tsim Sha Tsui	Retail
	New Town Plaza	Shatin	Residential
	City Plaza	Taikoo	Business
	Harbour City	Tsim Sha Tsui	Retail
	tmtplaza	Tuen Mun	Residential
	Lee Theatre	Causeway Bay	Retail
	World Trade Center	Causeway Bay	Retail
	Telford	Kowloon Bay	Residential
B+	Festival Walk	Kowloon Tong	Residential
	apm	Kwun Tong	Residential
	Maritime Square	Tsing Yi	Residential
B	Tai Po Megamall	Tai Po	Residential
	City Walk	Tsuen Wan	Residential
	Olympian City	Olympian City	Residential
	East Point City	Hang Hau	Residential
	Plaza Hollywood	Diamond Hill	Residential

Data are based on the average total sales of those stores by the end of 2011, created by the author.

ranking and does not necessarily depend on sales. Eight stores were ranked as A, some located in residential areas. Three stores were ranked as B+- and five as B-. This ranking is informal rather than personal, as the ranking was agreed to by many of the local employees.

The first major criterion of this ranking was the consumption power produced by the rent. Locations such as Harbor City in Tsim Sha Tsui and Lee Theatre in Causeway Bay are considered high-rent areas. Harbor City is one of the largest shopping malls in the major retail district. According to a Harbor City report, 2011 retail sales reached HK$3 billion, a growth of 22% (Harbor City, 2011: 16). The shopping mall offers a large number of worldwide brands, such as Gucci, ZARA, and Chanel. The rents and size of the apparel companies have grown by 32.8% and 29.9%, respectively, while rents have risen by around 30% to 40% each year (Harbor City, 2011: 20). Despite the mall's high rents, it has achieved 97% coverage, and around 25% of the companies renew their contract every year (Harbor City, 2011: 21). Local media reported that the last space has been leased to Italian brand Giorgio Armani, for a monthly HK$10 million, or HK$700 per square foot ("*Jidu qiangshou*" 2012). The data indicate that 30% of the customers are from mainland China ("*Haigangcheng*" 2011). The CEO of the Miramar shopping mall has also announced that rent has increased by around 20% ("*Meilihua*" 2013). The rent in the City Plaza in Taikoo has also increased, and almost all of the companies have renewed their contracts there (Singtao, 2001).

Local employees believe that this informal store ranking has influenced their promotions since store rankings and the career paths of Store Managers are interrelated. To manage stores well and achieve high investments and sales, experienced Store Managers were assigned to work at A-rank stores. This did not necessarily mean that higher-ranked employees at B+ ranked stores had no experience; only their skill levels were lower than those of Store Managers at the A-rank stores. In fact, this was just for promotion purposes. Higher-ranked employees at an A-rank store would usually work at a B-rank store first. The ideal career path for a non-management-trainee was starting at higher-ranked stores, where they could work with experienced colleagues, and then proceeding to lower-ranked stores after being promoted to higher positions, where they had fewer competitors and more time to learn new skills. In general, junior Store Managers were assigned to B-rank stores to gain experience and then moved up to upper-ranked stores. However, the unpredictable labor force in the retail industry led to some exceptions. For instance, one store manager started at an A-rank store because of a labor shortage.

Head Office

Now let us turn to the structure of the head office to illustrate how its detachment from the stores resulted in the latter's strong independence. I will examine the vertical relationship between the CEO of the Hong Kong region and office departments, the horizontal structure of the departments, and the office-store relationship.

As Figure 3.2 shows, all head office was under the command of the CEO of the Hong Kong region, and there was no direct department that formally controlled all the stores since all departments were expected to support store operations.

The vertical relationships among the CEO of Ichi Hong Kong, Zhang Peng, and the office departments centralized authority in Zhang, while his frequent absences resulted in the decentralization of power in favor of the departments or the offices' functional units. His position in Ichi prevented him from spending sufficient time supervising the Hong Kong operation and required him to pursue the standardization of the system. From October 2010 to November 2011, Zhang often had to fly between Hong Kong and mainland China (where he was the sole CEO), and his responsibility increased after his April 2011 promotion from Group Senior Vice President to Vice President and Executive of Ichi's mother company. Although his responsibility on the mainland was shared with the Chief Operating Officer (COO) as of November 2011, Zhang was still the sole CEO of Hong Kong until April 2012, when a COO was assigned to the position. The market factor was also important in the issue of the limited time of Zhang's visit. Unlike operations on the mainland, sales and new openings in Hong Kong increased stably; therefore, aside from meeting with the store manager once a month and making several store visits, he spent most of his time in mainland China.

Office departments with different functions are horizontally structured with decentralized power. There are six departments: the Store Operations Department, Merchandising Department, Marketing Department, Finance Department, Human Resources Department, and Ichi University. By the end of 2012, these had all been established at the Head Office of Ichi Hong Kong under the supervision of the Hong Kong CEO (see Figure 3.2). Working in the same company, office employees are reluctant to support store operations

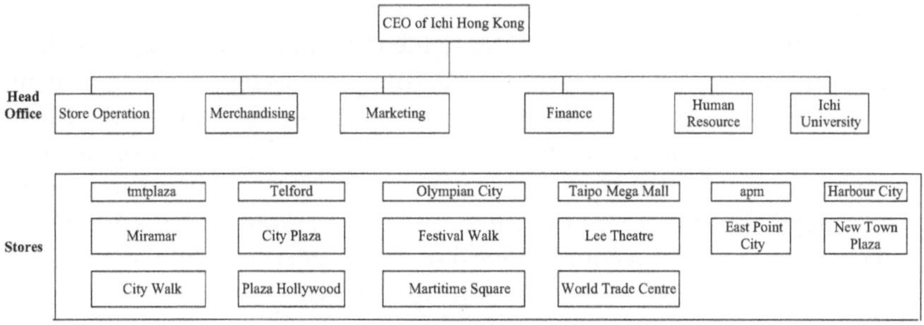

Figure 3.2 Hierarchy of head office and stores, Ichi, Hong Kong, 2011, created by the author.

by discussing their store experience and the intention of the directors. I will also point out why employees who worked in the Store Operations Department failed to support the store sufficiently and equally.

The Human Resources Department is responsible for recruitment, training, salary, and other related issues. The Department is led by the local Director, Mary, who has long experience with international retailers such as Marks and Spencer and the large Japanese retailer AEON. By the end of 2011, she was ranked second highest among all local department directors. Her limited store experience and harsh attitude to employees were criticized. Most Store Managers claimed that Mary relied on the "gossip" of local store employees to judge the work performance of Store Managers and that she tended to ignore the company system's fundamental problems. For instance, Mary claimed that the labor shortage was caused by the store manager's improper management without considering the possibility of a less localized human resources system. Several Store Managers argued that the labor structure of the store's part-timer-focused model, introduced by Ichi Japan, did not suit Hong Kong's early market situation. This problem was not solved until early 2011 when the Department finally announced a change to the full-timer-focused model.

The Merchandising Department is responsible for tasks such as the sales plan, inventory control, and weekly delivery. Store managers used to be allowed to contact the Merchandising Department directly to adjust the deliveries; however, they were asked to follow the department's instructions. The Merchandising Department is directed by Elaine, a local employee who has worked at the company for more than five years and was the most highly ranked employee in Hong Kong, including Japanese expatriates, at the end of 2012. Like the Director of Human Resources, Elaine had no experience working for Ichi and was reluctant to communicate with employees, even during the monthly store manager meeting. A Japanese store manager said that, although Elaine had a great ability to make plans, as she always grasped the essence of a standardized plan, she ignored too much of the store's reality. After a former local Supervisor was relocated to this Department, many Store Managers appreciated his "empathy," since his plans took more of the store's situation into consideration.

The functions of the Finance Department include accounting, budget preparation, financial policy formulation, and purchasing. The department frequently receives applications from the Supervisors (who support the Store Managers) about the replacement or maintenance of damaged tools such as whiteboards and cash registers. When the department receives many applications, they have discretion over which are most appropriate or worthwhile based on the standard procedure. A local store manager once told me that the Finance Department was quite reluctant to deal with the replacement issue and that department staff tended to accuse store employees of being careless because the equipment needed to be replaced too often.

The Marketing Department is responsible for company promotion and the weekly VMD instruction on window displays and full-body mannequins at the stores. The weekly instruction covers issues such as product codes, the color and size of outers, trousers, types of belts, and shoes. The department's main job is following the standard VMD plan for window displays. According to some local store employees, department staff regularly checked the store's VMD and made adjustments; however, I did not see them during my fieldwork (from the middle of 2010 to the end of 2011). This Department has less direct contact with the stores than other departments.

Ichi University provides training in management principles and the company philosophy to store employees, especially Management Trainees, and translates the company manual from Japanese to Traditional Chinese. The company's manuals have been standardized and form the basis of the written promotion examination. The department has spent more time training Management Trainees to satisfy Ichi headquarters' request that the number of Store Managers be increased and that they are encouraged, or "pushed," to become Store Managers within half a year. A local employee, Benjamin, is the chief of this department. He used to work as a Supervisor. In March 2011, he was assigned to this department. He ranks lower than the above-mentioned directors. Although Benjamin worked as a Supervisor before being relocated to this department, many Store Managers claimed that he has limited knowledge of store operations.

The Store Operation Department is the major mediator between the stores and the office. The higher-ranked employee and actual leader of the Store Operation Department were Mizuno. Office employees work on issues with the delivery, cleaning company, landlord, maintenance, customer service, and so on. Supervisors managed store operations by supporting the Store Managers, as Mizuno was not able to fully supervise operations regularly because of his busyness. Supervisory visits and informal store rankings were interrelated.

Each Supervisor was in charge of one area, comprising four to six variously ranked stores. Because of the company pursued high-cost performance, the number of Supervisors was limited, and most felt the effects of this labor shortage. Therefore, they had to prioritize the stores, as they had no time to regularly visit all of them. For instance, a local Supervisor was assigned to open a new store while also needing to manage seven other stores – three A-rank stores, one B+-store, and three B stores. Within half a year, he could manage to visit the EPC store every one or two months. A similar situation was obtained with the other B-ranked stores.

The priority of the store might not be the only reason for a lack of visits. However, visit frequency had a huge influence on the employees. For instance, because the EPC store Supervisor, Mark, seldom visited, many employees commented that they had been abandoned or neglected not only by the Supervisor but also by the company. By contrast, employees at the

A-rank store often met their Supervisor and thus confirmed their position in the market. Several weeks after a Full-time Salesperson was relocated to an A-rank store from the EPC store, she commented that the attitude of Mark was unexpectedly friendly and that she felt the store was important because of Mark's frequent visits.

It is interesting to notice that the office employees' reluctance concerning store operations and their limited store experience helped the stores gain independence from the office. Departments in the office were horizontally structured with specific functions without any official job rotation among departments which to some extent resulted in their detachment. Some department directors emphasized the importance of standardization rather than adjusting their practices and policies to local situations so they did not find necessary to look into the real situation. Moreover, many office employees believed that the Store Operations Department was responsible for taking care of store operations. However, employees, especially Supervisors in the Store Operations Department, were so busy and self-interested that unequal and insufficient supervision resulted, in transferring significant authority to the stores, especially to lower-ranked ones.

Conclusion

In this chapter, I have first analyzed the economic background of Ichi in Hong Kong and the implementation of its corporate ideology in the local market. I then used an ethnographical analysis of the organizational structure of the EPC store, the informal store rankings, and office-store relationships to investigate the stores' strong independence.

I have argued that the marketing strategy of offering products according to four key concepts (i.e., high value-added, reasonable prices, a wide range of customers, and high quality) and the location strategy designed to attract mainland Chinese tourists, as well as local residents, contributed significantly to Ichi Hong Kong's high sales volume. Ichi's DNA initially contributed little to its success. However, Ichi's development in Hong Kong was distinctive, as the company attempted to increase its managerial power by reinforcing the standardization of its DNA. This practice was introduced during a gradual growth in Hong Kong sales, which the company regarded as the result of over-localization and addressed after the announcement of the "Global One" policy.

To offer a general picture of the company's on-site practice, I examined the organizational chart of the company's fundamental units – the stores and the head office – to illustrate the different degrees of discretion exercised by the Store Managers. The case of the EPC store revealed that the stores had no formal structure and that the Store Managers made the final decisions about general operational issues. The decentralized powers of the Store Managers differed according to the informal store rankings, with lower-ranked stores enjoying greater independence through a lower status. Moreover, this hierarchy has influenced employees' notions of the ideal career path. The head office's structure revealed a detached relationship between the head office and the stores, which somewhat increased Store Managers' discretionary power over store operations.

In the next chapter, I will provide an overall image of a day's work at the EPC store to describe the employees' working lives and draw out the major research findings of this book.

Notes

1 Hong Kong's CSD explains that the traditional Four Key Industries in Hong Kong – financial services, trading and logistics, tourism, and professional and producer services – have been the key factors in Hong Kong's economic growth (CSD, 2013(a): 1).
2 Standardized stores are around 750 m^2 while large-scale ones are around 1,500–3,000 m^2.
3 Interview with Mizuno on September 25, 2010.
4 Interview with Mizuno on January 14, 2011.

Reference List

Aoki, M. (1986) Horizontal vs. Vertical Information Structure of the Firm. *The American Economic Review*, 76(5), pp. 971–983.

Aoki, M. (1990) Toward an Economic Model of the Japanese Firm. *Journal of Economic Literature*, 28(1), pp. 1–27.

Aoki, M. (1992) Decentralization-Centralization in Japanese Organization: A Dual Principle. In Kumon, S. and Rosovsky, H. (eds.), *The Japanese Political Economy (Vol. 3)*, pp. 142–69. Stanford, CA: Stanford University Press.

Census and Statistics Department, HKSAR. (2013(a)) *Feature Article: The Four Key Industries and Other Selected Industries in the Hong Kong Economy*. Hong Kong Monthly Digest of Statistics; CSD; Hong Kong Special Administrative Region, 15 Apr, 2013. PDF file.

Fan, I., & Yim, J. (2011) *Economic Focus: Hong Kong Tourism Industry. Hong Kong Still Has That Appeal With International Retailers*. Colliers International. Available at: https://www.hangseng.com/cms/tpr/eng/analyses/PDF/ecof_e_2011apr.pdf

'IMF External Relations Department' *People's Republic of China—Hong Kong Special Administrative Region—Preliminary Conclusions of the 2012 Article IV Mission*, 17 November, 2012. Available at: http://www.imf.org/external/np/ms/2012/111712.html (retrieved 25 Jun, 2013).

'HK Tops World's Retail Rent List' *ChinaDaily*, 15 November, 2012. Available at: http://www.chinadaily.com.cn/hkedition/2012-11/15/content_15930277.htm (retrieved 23 June, 2013).

'Hong Kong's Causeway Bay Tops Shop Rent List: Survey' *Agence France Presse*, 16 November 2012. Available at: http://www.scmp.com/news/hong-kong/article/1083879/hong-kongs-cause (retrieved 24 June, 2013).

Leung, P. 'More than 50 Global Retail Brands Set Up Shop in Hong Kong in 2012' *South Morning China*, 8 May, 2013. Available at: http://www.scmp.com/property/hong-kong-china/article/1232393/more-50-global-retail-brands-set-shop-hong-kong-2012 (retrieved 24 June, 2013).

'Mainland Tourists Tripling the Size of Hong Kong Population'. *Nielsen*, 21 February, 2011. Available at: http://hk.nielsen.com/news/20110221.shtml (retrieved 25 June, 2013).

Martin, M.F. (2007) Hong Kong: Ten Years after the Handover. *Foreign Affairs, Defense, and Trade Division*, *Congressional Research Service*. Available at: https://fas.org/sgp/crs/row/RL34071.pdf .

Nanto, D. (1998) CRS Report. The Asian (Global?) Financial Crisis, the IMF, and Japan: Economic Issues, *Congressional Research Service*. Available at: https://www.everycrsreport.com/files/19980903_98-434_a5e6deec70b573f7ad017bba532e491a184a03cc.pdf.

Ruo, L. (2012) "Zhongguo dalu youke xiaofei jianshao xianggang shechipin xiaoshou tongbi xiahua 10%" [Decrease of the consumption by mainland Chinese tourists to 10%]. *Wallstreetcn*, 5 October, 2012. Available at: http://wallstreetcn.com/node/18869 (retrieved 24 June, 2013).

Yu, J. (2012) 'Hong Kong Still No.1 for Mainland Chinese Tourists' *South China Morning Post*, 13 November, 2012. Available at: http://www.scmp.com/news/hong-kong/article/1081729/hk-still-no-1-mainland-tourists (retrieved 24 June, 2013).

4 Touring the Store's Space and Sense of Place

In the previous chapter, I examined how Ichi achieved a high sales volume in the Hong Kong market in its early phase and how the company gradually began to stress the importance of its corporate ideology, or DNA. The organizational structure of the local subsidiary showed the flexibly structured stores and their high independency. To understand a spatial expression used by Ichi store workers, I will describe a day's work at the East Point City (EPC) store through my perspective as an intern, thus illustrating how employees are assigned to their tasks and how they behave on-site. This chapter also attempts to introduce the major arguments of the following chapters, focusing on Ichi's human resources system and institutional culture.

An Ichi workday is divided into three major chronological parts: morning preparation, opening hours, and closing preparation. After the environment of the EPC store is discussed, morning preparation will be described. This process comprises three phases: preparation before the work, opening preparation, and morning briefing. I will then show how employees are assigned during opening hours and after closing to describe the company's system and the influential elements of employees' work behavior.

Setting the EPC Store

The EPC store opened in a shopping mall in Hang Hau in 2007. The mall is located in a new town, Tseung Kwan O, in the southern part of Sai Kung District, Kowloon. Before touring the EPC store, I shall briefly describe its environment.

Tseung Kwan O, the seventh new town in Hong Kong, began developing in 1982 by reclaiming Tseung Kwan O Bay ("Tseung Kwan O", 2013). The first residents arrived in 1988, and the population increased to 436,627 by 2011 according to Hong Kong's Census and Statistic Department (CSD). The CSD also indicates that Sai Kung District's median monthly domestic household income was HK$26,870 in 2011, ranking third among 18 districts, after Wan Chai District and the Central and Western District. New Town in Tseung Kwan O was regarded as a suitable choice for local people who wanted to live close to the city on a limited budget. Considering the median monthly

DOI: 10.4324/9781003305675-4

domestic household income relative to housing types in Tseung Kwan O reveals the strong consumption power of residents in private housing and the gap with those in public rental housing. While residents in private, permanent housing receive around HK$40,000 monthly income, residents in public rental housing receive HK$12,640.

Let us look into the situation in Hang Hau. There are around 15 housing types close to this area, including three public housing projects – the Hau Tak Estate (厚德邨), Ming Tak Estate (明德邨), and the King Lam Estate (景林邨) – and large-scale private housing developments, including EPC (東港城), Nan Fung Plaza (南豐廣場), La Cite Noble (新寶城), and Maritime Bay (海悅豪園), linked together by pedestrian bridges. There are around seven more private housing developments near the Hang Hau metro station. There are educational institutions such as kindergartens, primary schools, and secondary schools near these buildings. Transportation in Hang Hau is convenient, as most residential buildings are close to the Hang Hau metro station, which began operating in August 2002, and other transportation methods are available, such as an overnight bus and minibus to other areas.

Now, I would like to describe the environment of the EPC shopping mall that houses Ichi. EPC was the first large-scale shopping arcade in downtown Tseung Kwan O. It is 400,000 square feet and is linked to the Hang Hau metro station. Other shopping malls are close to the EPC mall, such as Hauk Tak Shopping Centre (厚德商場) and The Lane (連理街). The mall had around 160 shops in 2010 including 50 brand-name fashion stores, over 20 cosmetics, and skin care shops, and more than 10 jewelry stores ("EPC", 2012).

EPC residents include a small middle class. As there are few mainland Chinese, the store has many local customers from the surrounding residential buildings.

The workday began in my apartment in Saiwan, the Western part of Hong Kong Island. It took around 50 minutes to one hour to go from my house to the EPC store. I usually took the bus near my residence directly to the North Point metro station. I then walked quickly to the metro station and took the Tseung Kwan O Line directly to the Hang Hau station. After getting off, I walked quickly toward the metro exit with the other passengers.

After passing the metro exit, I took the escalator to the first floor and then went across a local shopping mall that housed many relatively low-end local brands to reach the EPC mall. On my way to the store, I would see many passengers – mothers, domestic helpers with boys and girls, and elderly people. Once in the EPC mall, I would see many global and local brand shops, such as Lafuma, FOOTSPOT, Cotton On, G2000, The Body Shop, Chow SangSang, and Marks & Spencer, which would still be closed.

Morning Preparation

I arrived 30 minutes before my work since I had to buy breakfast, and Ichi employees are required to arrive 15 minutes before they start preparing for the opening, 8:45 in my case. I then bought breakfast at KFC, a nearby bakery, or a market downstairs for a change. After buying breakfast, I went to the toilet, as I did not want to go during the morning preparation. At 8:44, I passed the fashion brand, ESPRIT, arrived at the store, pushed a button to open the plastic shutter, and went inside.

The EPC store housed five different blocks (A block to E block), one fitting room, one cash register corner, one back room, one staff room (combined with the manager's room), and one alternation room (see Figure 4.1). There were two entrances, one inside C block and another inside A block. Although space was limited, the store had as many products as in a larger store. In general, A block housed products for women, B block had underwear, C block had men's clothing, D block had jeans and pants, and E block had kids' products and men's underwear. Most of the highly popular women's and men's items were kept in C block.

While walking through the shop floor, I greeted every staff with a smile, and some of them smiled back. I knocked on the staff room door before entering, as all employees were asked to do. I saw Patrick, a male part-timer, and Annjo, a female part-timer. We greeted each other, and I put my bag in the locker.

At 8:48, I ate quickly while writing down the top five items sold and other notices, trying to finish within the remaining 12 minutes. I had a quick look at the whiteboard announcing the top five items, the number of top five sold, the previous day's sales, and today's sales target. That day's top five were the women's heatech V-neck T-shirt (eight lengths), the flannel check long-sleeve shirt, the premium down jacket, the women's fleece full zip jacket, and the down jacket. I used abbreviations such as "pre" to indicate "premium"

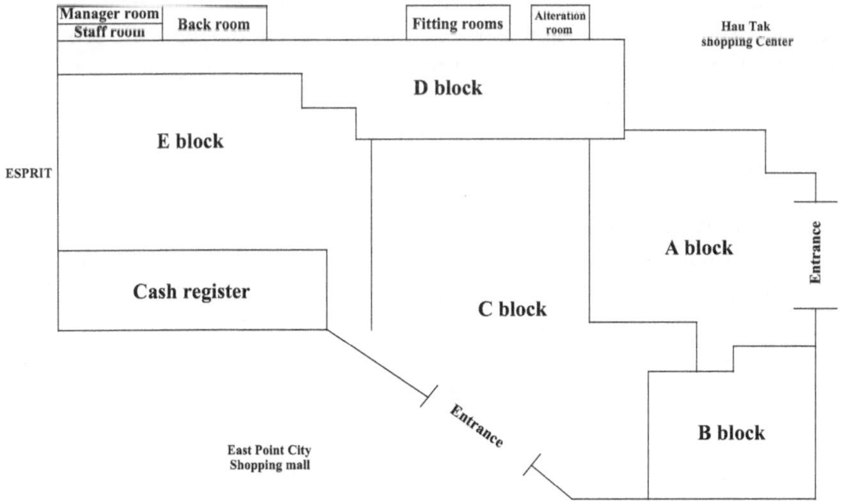

Figure 4.1 Store layout of EPC store, 2011, created by the author.

and "jk" to indicate "jacket" to save time. I then checked the bulletin board for other notices like the weekly store policies or the Supervisor's report. There were none that day, so I was able to make a full note of every important point before work began.

Another important task was checking the daily work schedule hung on the left side of the staff room wall. Patrick and Annjo complained about their schedule. Patrick said that he was again assigned to work at both C block and A block in one day. People working at C block and A block were informally required to greet customers as loudly as possible. Patrick was once assigned to C block for three hours, and his throat became very painful. When Patrick found that he had to work at C block for three hours again that day, he was furious. Annjo was lucky that day to be assigned to work at a cash register, the fitting room, and D block because these jobs were less "boring (as she said)," and she could even chat with colleagues. Moreover, working in those places made one somewhat "superior" to other part-timers since new and junior part-timers were seldom assigned to them. Patrick also complained that the Store Manager Jenny sometimes selfishly revised his break time to be able to chat with him.

I looked at my schedule and was relieved to find that I did not have to do the cleaning before opening anymore. This task had been assigned to a new part-timer, but, since we had no new part-timers, I had been responsible for this task for more than three months. I might call myself a cleaning expert.

At 8:58, Annjo screamed because she had almost forgotten to punch the clock. At 8:59, we put on our neck-strap holders with our name cards and wrapped our black waist pouches around our waists; the pouches contained scissors, a small notebook, pens, a cutter, the Staff Manual, measuring tape, and a strip of cloth. At 9:00, we left the staff room and went to our locations.

I was assigned to replenish B block's lamb's wool and heatech products and fetch two other carbon boxes of products. While I was replenishing the products, I saw the Store Manager, Jenny, walk by and tell Cathy, a female Full-time Salesperson, to work faster in A block. Cathy came toward B block and whispered,

> You know, the Store Manager at my previous store is really nice! She is good at her work. She told us a lot of things, and importantly, she is a funny person! I really like working with her! I was transferred here because they lack employees, but here, I have learned nothing. It is close to my house, so the location is good, but... I want to learn more. Jenny, she is not good at her work, she always says that she does not have enough time to teach us, but I don't believe her.

Apart from the Store Manager Jenny's poor job skills, employees were afraid that their insufficient on-the-job training would slow their career progression within the company since skill mattered most for the promotion.

Senior Salesperson Kelvin came toward me an hour later and asked if I had already finished replenishment B block. He then assigned me to D block, where Annjo was replenishing wool sweaters, to help her replenish down jackets. Then Kelvin walked quickly to other blocks to check staff progress. I rarely saw Kelvin replenish stock but frequently saw him on the shop floor, while the Store Manager spent considerable time in the manager's room. When I was almost finished with my task, I saw Advanced Salesperson Janet check that all price pops were placed correctly. Then I saw her go to the alternation room to check that every product had been done. Advanced Salespersons rarely do front-line work such as replenishment but focus more on managerial work. At the EPC store, it was quite rare to see Store Manager Jenny on the shop floor; she usually stayed in the manager's room and dealt with work schedules and other paperwork.

While I was replenishing the products in D block, I overheard Kelvin consulting Jenny regarding the layout, based on one designed by Deputy Store Manager Michelle the day before. Kelvin believed that there had been inappropriate changes. While Kelvin proposed his idea to Jenny, she listened carefully and then said, "I understand your point. But I think this way is better." After hearing Jenny's comment, Kelvin said only, "OK." I then remembered that Kelvin once described Ichi as a military institution, in which subordinates basically had to follow their superiors' decisions.

At 10:35, Kelvin asked employees to leave their undone tasks and move all the products to the back room. After doing this, we went to the staff room to get our walkie-talkies and earphones in preparation for the opening hour. After taking the walkie-talkies and putting them in our waist pouches, we walked toward the cash registers, while chatting with each other. Although we were not able to finish replenishing that day, employees were quite relaxed, since they had left their undone work to their colleagues.

At 10:45, we stood in a line facing Kelvin, the Store Manager Jenny, and the Advanced Salesperson Janet. Two security guards stood next to us. Today's host was Kelvin, who said, "Good morning, everyone", indicating the start of the morning briefing. He checked if we had our walkie-talkies and earphones. Then the higher-ranked employees checked for the "Ichi Style" ensuring that employees' appearance fit Ichi's requirements, including the proper placement of our neck strip holder and name card, the cleanliness of our shoes, nails, hair style and color, and accessories. Roy, who wore white Converse shoes, was asked to clean them because they were dirty. I was relieved that my nails were not too long and that their color was sufficiently simple. The "Ichi Style" allowed for individual differences. I saw Jenny ask Queenie, a new part-timer, to take off her big black earrings: they were apparently not "Ichi-like," though the company manual does not indicate this. Then, the male employees were required to raise their hands so that Kelvin could check if their underwear would appear. Kelvin also checked if we were wearing wristwatches.

After we named the top five items and the numbers sold yesterday, the briefing session moved on to the core part, the chorus of the "Three Promises", the "Ichi Basic Policy", and the "Six Magic Words", all focusing on customer-related issues and job efficiency; for instance, the company expected store employees to be polite and honest with customers. The Six Magic Words were words the company encouraged store employees to use during interactions with customers to improve CS and the Ichi brand.

Some part-timers seemed confused because higher-ranked employees had rarely required employees to chant the first two choruses. When Kelvin asked a new part-timer, Queenie, to lead the chorus, she answered that she had not memorized the first two chants. Kelvin then asked another part-timer, Annjo, who had more experience. Once Annjo has chanted the first sentence, we followed and bowed together. When Annjo got to the second sentence of the Ichi Basic Policy, she could not remember the rest. Therefore, a Full-time Salesperson, Roy, was asked to lead the chorus and finished successfully. Although we were supposed to keep the basic posture and smile with the corners of our mouths curved up during the chorus, no staff at the EPC store, even full-timers, did so.

During Opening Hours

I was assigned to B block, cash register, break, cleaning, A block, and fitting room during opening hours. This was not unpleasant, since I could work at different locations. I was glad to find that I would be working at the cash register and fitting room, where I found that time passed quickly.

At 11:00 am, I was ready at B block. Twenty minutes after the store opened, a customer came toward my block and looked into the popular items. We were encouraged to walk toward customers and give them suggestions whenever the store's sales were poor, although this went against Ichi's self-service principle, which allowed customers to shop without interacting with employees. As the store's sales were good at the time, I continued walking. The customer asked me loudly whether the M size fit her. I told her that she could determine this by referring to her chest circumference. She told me that she had no idea of her chest circumference and only used inches, not centimeters. She asked me if it was possible to measure her chest since she could not try the item on. I took out the measuring tape and indicated her size. We were obliged to tell customers clearly that underwear could not be refunded or returned. Another female customer approached me and asked me about the size of some leggings. The waist and hip sizes were shown clearly on the package but in Japanese. I asked her size and gave her a suggestion.

After working at B block for two hours, I had to move to the next destination, E block (with the cash register). This task required staff to work in E block and help with the cash register when necessary. Therefore, employees who were assigned to this task needed to have cashier skills.

When I arrived, I saw two part-timers, Faye and Glendy, chatting at the cash register. Since there were few customers at that time, I moved to E block to fold products.

I soon saw some customers waiting in line, so I went to the cash register to help them. While inputting my employee number, I repeatedly told myself not to make a mistake since we were required to pay for any losses. Then I raised my hands to show that my cash register was available by saying, "Next customer, please!" After the customer came to me, I counted the number of products and gave the customer the total owed for the products. When I noticed underwear products, I told the customer that these products were not refundable and that she had to make sure that they fit. I also saw a woolen item, so I explained how to wash it. Then I said that, if she wanted to return a product, she could bring the receipt to any store within 30 days. At this time, I realized that I had forgotten to take the security device off the wool product. After collecting the Visa card from the customer, I waited for the purchase to go through. When I passed the receipt to the customer, I confirmed that the total amount of money on the Visa receipt and the store's receipt was the same and that I did not overcharge the customer. I gave her the Visa card with both hands and thanked her for coming. The whole procedure finished within one to two minutes that day; however, it took some time before I learned how to finish quickly without making mistakes.

At 14:00, my colleagues and I had a late lunch. Six employees took their breaks with me. The Store Manager and Senior Salesperson prepared to have lunch in the staff room, while three of us, Cathy, Janet, and I, went to the nearest restaurant. After we all got our order, Janet began to complain that the Store Manager's job skills were poor and that she wanted to be relocated and work with more experienced Store Managers. Cathy agreed, and they were excited about this topic. They also said that it was the Senior Salesperson's social skills that allowed him to be promoted rather than his actual job skill. Cathy said that, although he always smiled at his superiors, he always gave her a *hak min* ("poker face" in Cantonese).

After we arrived at the store 15 minutes before work, some of us rested in the staff room while others talked with their friends. Five minutes before work, we chanted the Six Magic Words.

The assignments for my afternoon shift were cleaning, A block, and the fitting room. On my way to the back room, I saw Patrick and Annjo replenishing the stock from the blue box when I recalled that the Store Operation Department's new policy did not allow more than one person to do the replenishing during opening hours since store employees were supposed to spend more time on customer service. It did not feel strange to see this, since EPC store operations were controlled by the Store Manager. I entered the back room to take the mop, which might not have been cleaned for a relatively long time.

While I was mopping the floor, I saw two familiar faces near the entrance in A block – Mizuno, the Operations Manager, and Mark, the local

Supervisor. At the same time, I saw Janet, the Advanced Salesperson, who was checking the replenishment progress in A block, announce "Boss" (*daai lou* in Cantonese) quietly into her walkie-talkie so that the employees who were replenishing with blue boxes would bring them to the back room as quickly as possible. I soon heard two part-timers rush toward the back room with blue boxes. Although Janet assumed that Mizuno and Mark might have already seen the situation, she had to at least pretend to actually care about company regulations.

As Mizuno and Mark entered the store, I suddenly heard employees greeting very loudly. I was surprised and looked around. Part-timers who had been working without energy a minute before suddenly "revived" and greeted as loudly as possible. There were many male part-timers that day, and their voices resonated in the store. While being impressed by their greeting abilities, I heard the loud greetings of some full-timers who usually did not greet, such as Kelvin, and I saw Jenny, who rarely came out of the staff room, start to greet the others. I naturally followed their practice and started greeting them loudly.

I went back to the back room to store the mop. When I came out, fewer employees greeted when I realized that Mizuno and Mark had already left. I was surprised since they only stayed at the store for less than an hour. It might be because they had to focus more on a new opening store. On my way to A block, I bumped into a full-timer who said me that Mark had not come to the store for more than two months and he had already 'abandoned' the EPC store.

I saw a new female part-timer, Serena, in A block and I then took over from her. While I was replenishing the stock, I saw a female customer carrying three products in her arms. I grabbed a shopping basket immediately and handed it to her as the company requires. She said, "Thank you" in Mandarin. Twenty minutes later, Roy, the Full-time Salesperson, said, "The mystery shopper wants to talk to you. She is in B block. By the way, she speaks Mandarin." I recalled that a new practice called "CS Checkup" had started. When I arrived at B block, I saw a woman taking an iPhone photo of a male part-timer, William, who was holding his name card on the shop floor. William was behaving as if he had done something terrible. I suddenly recalled that she was the one to whom I had passed the shopping basket. I thought she might write positively about me since I had done this, a basic CS requirement. I thus gave her permission to take my photo. We then spoke:

MYSTERY SHOPPER: When you were replenishing the stock there, who was standing next to you?

I: There was no one standing next to me.

MYSTERY SHOPPER: I am sure that there was someone standing next to you.

I: What does that person look like?

MYSTERY SHOPPER: Let me find the picture [searching in her iPhone]...I cannot find it. Just forget about it.

I could not understand the intent of her question, but I felt it might be something wrong. Moreover, I had not talked to anyone while replenishing the stock. I denied that I had but had no proof. The mystery shopper left the store without offering comments or feedback to the Store Manager although she wrote a long report. After the mystery shopper left, William told me that she took a photo of him because he had been chatting with Serena, the girl who was replenishing the stock before me at A block. I assumed that the mystery shopper had confused me with Serena, which was unlikely because Serena looked very different from me: my hair is brown, and hers is black; she was also wearing black while I was wearing white that day.

While still confused about the mystery shopper's behavior, I moved to the next assigned location, the fitting room. This had a small counter that took alteration requests and several fitting rooms. My partners were the new part-timer, Lois, a vocational school student, and the Full-time Salesperson, Cathy, who had long experience working for apparel companies and had never had a customer complaint at the EPC store. We were glad to be assigned to the fitting room, where we could chat with colleagues. Although it was one of the best working locations in the store, employees, including me, sometimes felt helpless there, especially during peak season, where we were that day.

I was responsible for controlling the number of items customers took into the room. If they wanted to try on more than was allowed, I kept the rest of the products in the basket and placed it on the shelf at the counter; Cathy then brought them to the room. Lois was responsible for maintaining the cleanliness of each room. We collaborated well at the beginning; however, the situation became messy as more customers came to request alterations. Cathy went to take care of a male customer wanting a hem taken up. When another customer made the same request, I asked the new part-timer to take care of it since I had to take care of the counter; however, she had not learned how to do this task. Therefore, I took the hem for the customer while Lois worked at the counter. While Cathy and I were busy handling alternations, female customers asked us to bring products in other colors and sizes for them. Lois called for help by walkie-talkie, but no one answered or helped us. We could only ask customers to wait, though they rushed us many times. After finishing her task, Cathy ran to the shop floor to get the customers' products. Her long experience working at Ichi came in handy; otherwise, it would have taken a long time for a new part-timer to find the products.

I worked with Cathy and Lois for several hours, and it was time to move to the A block. My target that day was to finish organizing all products within the block within two hours after the closing.

Closing Preparation

Fifteen minutes before the closing, no staff was greeting, since everyone was focused on finishing their tasks on time. Two customers remained on the shop floor when Sabrina, the Senior Salesperson, closed one of the shutters. The customers looked at their watches and left rapidly.

Sabrina and the Management Trainee Gina were responsible for the closure preparations that day. Sabrina assigned us tasks in various areas. It was surprisingly quiet in the store, unlike during the morning preparation. Night shift higher-ranked employees pushed employees to finish on time since they had to make sure the shop floor was organized, allowing the morning shift employees to finish replenishing. Moreover, if employees worked overtime, higher-ranked employees had to write a report explaining the cause, which they preferred to avoid.

I was assigned to A block, which contained many popular items. I really disliked this block because it was always chaotic. I pushed myself to finish my task without neglecting *kijun* (standard) on the shop floor because Sabrina was quite serious about this. She did not want any of us to hinder her promotion, which was partly based on the performance of the standard of the shop floor at night. She had failed last time because of the low standard displayed on the shop floor at night. I saw Sabrina walking around the shop floor, checking everybody's work, which she rarely did otherwise.

While I was busy folding products, I saw Gina collecting money from the cash registers. I realized that this was the first time I had seen her on the shop floor. Sabrina came toward me and complained that Gina rarely helped us but was busy doing nothing in the staff room the whole night. According to Sabrina, Gina's poor effort forced her to do Gina's work. Moreover, Gina was supposed to be handing out the assignments because of her higher rank; however, Sabrina, who was two ranks lower, had to do this task instead.

After folding thousands of products, we finally finished our work. Sabrina closed the shutter, and then we ran to the metro station to catch the last metro. On the way to the metro through the EPC mall and another shopping mall, I found that all the other stores had already closed. A full-timer said, "You know, Ichi employees are the first ones to come and the last to leave." Since my apartment was not directly connected to the metro station, I had to transfer a bus or minibus from Central station to my place. Most full-timers took a minibus or metro, while some part-timers walked home. If we were too late to catch a bus or metro, we had to take a taxi instead, which cost more than HK$150 to my place and was generally ineligible for reimbursement.

Conclusion

In this chapter, I first analyzed the environment of the EPC store, located in a new town area and patronized mostly by local customers in Hong Kong's middle-income range. I then described a day's work from my point of view, proceeding chronologically from the opening preparation, going through opening hours, and ending with the closing preparation. My observations were intended to outline several arguments that I will explore in this book. I am going to touch on four issues: the training of multifunctional workers, the relationship between rank and assignments, momentary evaluations and collaborative performance, and the differences among interpretations of the Ichi ideology driven by variations among Store Managers.

One of the distinctive features of Ichi's work was the multifunctionality of employee skills, which I will explore in Chapters 5 and 6. Ambiguous job classifications caused a flexible job rotation. Employees were rotated frequently among different tasks based on the skills they had gained through their rotation. The job assignments of those with wider skill ranges had greater variety. With their multifunctional workers, the store could deal with problems quickly and efficiently, such as in the example of the fitting room. Moreover, many tasks overlapped, and employees of various ranks might perform the same task, even when the task was unrelated to their rank.

To assess the degree to which employees had learned Ichi-specific skills, the visits of the mystery shopper and the superior were described and illustrated the less objective assessment of the mystery shopper and the "immediate" collaborative presentation during the superior's visit. These points will be discussed in detail in Chapter 7. The mystery shopper confused what she *thought* she saw with what she *actually* saw, resulting in a less objective assessment. A follow-up with the mystery shopper also indicated that the company used her to managerially control the local employees without considering the possibility of a distorted assessment. In her final report, the mystery shopper praised a male part-timer for something he had not done and negatively evaluated employees without firm proof. Although the EPC store's local Store Manager claimed that the result had been distorted, Japanese and local superiors found that her attitude was inappropriate since her assessment was designed to maintain objectivity. The superior's visit showed how store employees immediately and "collaboratively" displayed their CS practice.

Though the employees seemed collaborative, they also had conflicts because of their self-interest. Their differences were strongly influenced by their Store Managers. I have pointed out in this chapter that the Store Managers' reluctance influenced worker motivation. I will show in Chapter 8 how five Store Managers created various "regimes" due to their different career orientations and managerial control methods to illustrate the significant role Store Managers play in company operations.

In the next chapter, I will examine how Ichi designed its training program and rotation formula to produce multifunctional workers and thus enhance cost performance on the shop floor.

References

'East Point City' 2012. Available at: http://www.eastpointcity.com.hk/en/home/ (retrieved 20 June, 2013).

'Tseung Kwan O New Town' *Civil Engineering and Development Department*. The Government of the Hong Kong Special Administrative Region, 1 January, 2013. Available at: http://www.cedd.gov.hk/eng/about/achievements/regional/regi_tko.html (retrieved 26 Jul, 2013).

5 Ichi Training and Identity Formation

One of the crucial issues for both employers and front-line employees is skill development (Koike, 1984). Kazuo Koike points out that one characteristic of the skill formation of workers in the Japanese factory is their frequent job rotation (1984: 48). He argues that the relationship between their seniority and their wages is logical, as employees who have worked longer for their company have more skills and deserve higher wages (Koike, 1984: 69–70). Masahiko Aoki illustrates this point by arguing that the Japanese firm has a distinctly decentralized information system (1992), in which employees are required to have "general and versatile" knowledge rather than "specialized expertise," enabling each work unit to adapt to the situation and modify the plan set by the central authority (Aoki, 1992: 149).

Echoing the argument of Koike and Aoki, I will describe Ichi's skill formation process in this chapter by taking the East Point City (EPC) store as an example, leaving the discussion of ranking and wages for the next chapter. I will describe how each task is classified vaguely, resulting in flexible assignments. I then investigate in detail how store employees are rotated among different store tasks based on daily work schedule data. After analyzing intra-store rotation, I will describe the inter-store and office-store job rotations to illustrate the importance of skill formation to employees' career development.

Managerial Work and Front-Line Work

As mentioned in the last chapter, jobs at the EPC store were divided into managerial and front-line work. Employees assigned to managerial tasks supported the front-line employees while front-line work was closely related to direct interaction with customers. Managerial work was assigned only to experienced full-timers while front-line work was assigned to both full-timers and part-timers since the higher-ranked managerial work required a mastery of the front-line work. In what follows, I shall explain the nature of both the higher-ranked managerial and front-line work. Specific tasks were displayed on the daily work schedule, which was slightly different from the formal divisions defined by the store. In this chapter, I will combine the division of labor in the formal structure with that in the daily work schedule. As Store

DOI: 10.4324/9781003305675-5

Managers were highly autonomous, the number of managerial and front-line tasks and their employee selections varied among them. This chapter uses data drawn from the EPC store from March 2011 to August 2011.

Manager, one Assistant Store Manager, one Senior Salesperson, four Advanced Salespersons, and three Full-time Salespersons. Part-timers comprised 70% of store staff. By discussing the store's vague job classifications and job assignments, I am describing the distinctive feature of the basis of all store work, Ichi's manuals, and the relationship between employees' formal ranking and their assigned work tasks.

According to the daily work schedule, front-line work had seven different tasks: cash register, fitting room, sales floor, S/S (for *shōhin seiri*, meaning "organization of products"), visual merchandising display (VMD), alteration room, and back room. All these tasks were defined in the company's manuals. Managerial work included human resources, training, inventory control (men's, women's, and kids'), pops and stickers, check and assignment, and customer service (CS). The basic premise was that assigned employees were to master the knowledge required by front-line workers since managerial work was intended to support and enhance the efficiency of front-line work. The practice of CS was not written in the daily work schedule because employees were expected to practice it regardless of the kind of work they were assigned. Only employees working in the alteration room and the back room did not directly interact with customers.

Vague Demarcation of Work and Overlapping Work

There was no clear demarcation between tasks, as many overlapped. The work types had no official descriptions, in the way many early tasks were ambiguous and produced by fluid job classification (Aoki, 1990; Clark, 1979; Itoh, 1994; Wong, 1999). The tasks had to be based on the company's manuals rather than employees' own experiences. Therefore, Ichi preferred promoting full-time salespeople and part-timers rather than drawing mid-career candidates from outside the company. Moreover, each store had the authority to recruit when labor was short. When new employees joined the company, the job title on their name plates was simply either "Full-time Salesperson" or "Part-time Salesperson." Therefore, the company did not require any special skills from their new employees, who were supposed to learn everything later, from the details to the overall store operation.

Thus, employees were responsible for multiple tasks. Front-line workers had to perform many implicitly shared tasks; they had to do work to which they had not been formally assigned when necessary. The ambiguous boundaries between tasks meant that employees had to share many tasks with colleagues on a daily basis. For instance, employees on the shop floor might be asked to take tailored products to customers since there was no specific location for collecting products that had alterations. When workers were assigned to "RUN," colleagues working at the cash register, in the fitting room, or at another location would very likely need their help. Because of their work's flexibility, they were often asked to help customers.

To illustrate, I shall describe a case in which employees had to tend to their environment. D block and E block had to not only work at their blocks but also help when necessary (see Figure 5.1). D block mainly housed pants and jeans for men and women. To the right of the fitting rooms and to the left of the back room, there were men's pants. To the left of the fitting rooms, there were women's pants and jeans. Besides the products near the wall, other products, such as men's wear and shoes, were also kept in the block. As the figure shows, the fitting rooms were quite close to D block, so employees working there were expected to help with the fitting rooms when necessary.

Employees would help workers in the fitting room return the items to the sales floor, as some customers might choose only one product after trying on three; the customers did not have to return the unwanted products to the sales floor; the employees had to. The second task was finding products for customers wanting to try them while in the fitting room. The third task was copying receipts for customers when the pants they had bought for alterations were from other stores; employees had to go to the staff room to copy them for the customers. Employees working in E block also helped the cashiers because of the block's proximity. Although C block is also close to the cash registers, employees there had to stand at the entrance for attracting potential customers and were thus not able to help.

As with front-line work, most full-timers were assigned to more than two managerial tasks, except in inventory control. One Advanced Salesperson was assigned to five different tasks – human resources, training, inventory control (in the women's section), checks and assignments, and pops. Two other Advanced Salespersons, excluding the trainer of an inventory control section, were assigned to two and three tasks. Moreover, higher ranked employees had to take care of unwritten requirements, such as checking so-called "D-rank" problems such as empty hangers, the wrong order of hangers in a display, clothing on the floor, items without packing, and an accumulation of products. When higher-ranked employees checked the sales floor, they had to make sure that D-rank situations had been resolved. At the same time, they had to greet customers just like anybody else and help customers find their products when necessary.

The overlapping of work tasks indicates that differently ranked employees sometimes performed the same job; the limited size of the store and the labor shortage reinforced this flexibility (see Table 5.1). This finding echoes the early literature (Aoki, 1986, 1990; Wong, 1999). Wong finds a similar phenomenon in a Japanese company in Hong Kong and claims that this ambiguous classification helps the company make flexible assignments (1999: 92). Aoki claims that this flexibility is different from the practice in America, where superiors respect their workers' collective agreements and do not assign jobs beyond their terms (1990: 17–18).

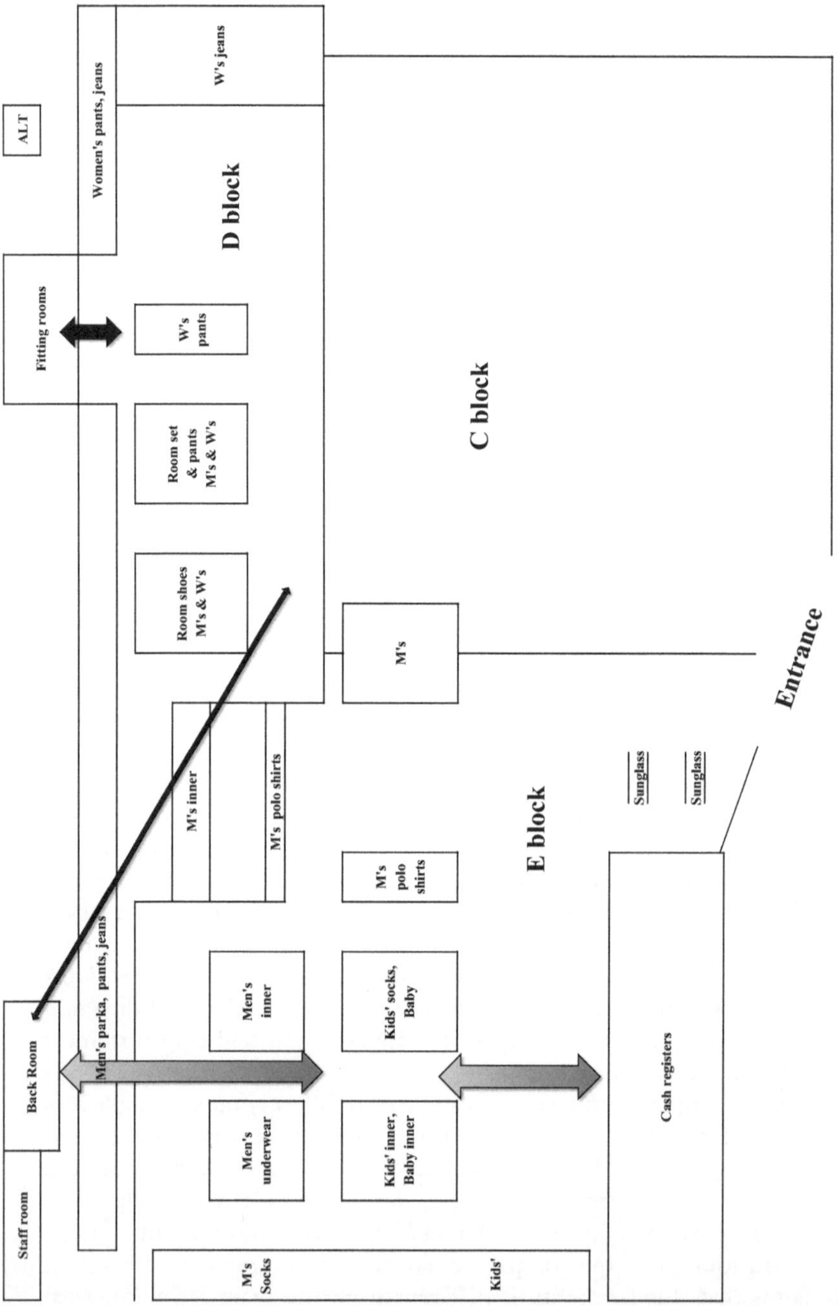

Figure 5.1 Tasks at D block and E block, EPC store, 2011, created by the author.

Table 5.1 Rank and assignment, Ichi, Hong Kong, EPC store, 2011

Work type	*Work contents*	*General assignment*
Managerial work	Check and assignment	Senior salespersons who were ranked above
	Human resource	All employees who were ranked above Advanced Salesperson
	Training	Advanced salesperson
	CS team	Assistant store manager, advanced salesperson, the full-time salesperson (good CS)
	Inventory control	Experienced full-time salesperson
Front-line work	Cash register	All employees with cashier skill
	Alternation	Full-time salesperson
	Visual merchandising display	
	Backroom	
	Change layout	Experienced part-timer, Full-time salesperson
	Organization of products (S/S)	Part-time, full-time salesperson
	RUN	
	Replenishment	
	Fitting room	
	A block, C block	
	E block	Part-timer
	Paste discount stickers	Part-timer
	Check item	
	D block, B block	New part-timer
	Cleaning	

Created by the author.

Thus, differently ranked employees perform similar tasks. The most common Ichi front-line task was working the cash register. Even employees not formally assigned to the work schedule were required to help the cashier when necessary. Other tasks were worked by both part-timers and full-timers, such as changing the layout, replenishment, the fitting room, A block, and C block. These tasks were more important than those reserved for junior part-timers. For instance, at least one experienced staff always worked in the fitting room to prevent customer complaints and increase purchase opportunities. Replenishment was rarely assigned to managers, who were higher than Advanced Salespersons at the EPC store unless the Store Manager required them to do so. Because of the labor shortage, some Advanced Salespersons even had to assist the senior salespeople, although this was also allowed in other stores. At some stores, such as the City Plaza store, where there were many higher-ranked employees, advanced salespersons were regarded as having more skills than full-time salespersons. Even so, they were not entitled to do the Senior Salesperson's job. The assignment of each work depended on the Store Manager rather than on company policy.

One task generally assigned to part-timers, phoning customers who had asked for a stock check, frequently attracted complaints. Even new part-timers were sometimes assigned to this work since the schedule-makers did not consider this work as important as the company did. As this task was not included in the intensive OJT, employees had to learn it from their superiors or colleagues after being assigned. I once was asked how to do it by a new part-timer in the staff room since he had received no OJT, unbelievably. Although alterations were usually assigned to full-timers at Ichi, the EPC and City Plaza store employee typically assigned this task was an experienced middle-aged woman part-timer. Because of her long years of service in a related industry, she had strong alteration skills, for which she had been hired. When she was off work, Full-time Salespersons or Advanced Salespersons took her place.

The higher-ranked managerial work was limited except in human resources. Senior higher-ranked employees were frequently assigned to checks and assignments while junior higher-ranked employees were responsible for training. Although the store expected experienced higher-ranked employees to improve operations through checks and assignments, lower-ranked employees could work on layouts and training, which directly influenced store operations and sales because of the employees' skills. This situation occurred at the EPC store because there were too few workers who could share tasks, for several possible reasons. The first is the labor structure, which emphasized part-timers and limited the number of managers. Another was the Store Manager's reluctance to arrange for OJT, which would have allowed junior higher-ranked employees and lower-ranked full-timers to learn managerial skills.

Differently ranked employees on the CS team also performed common tasks. Members included the Assistant Store Manager, who worked for less than a year, the Advanced Salesperson, and the Full-time Salesperson, who had worked at Ichi for more than two years. They evaluated each employee's CS practices. Another example involved an Advanced Salesperson who had worked at the company for more than three years and the Assistant Store Manager, who had been promoted from Management Trainee after less than a year. Because the Assistant Store Manager had little experience, the Advanced Salesperson had to do not only her job but the Assistant Store Manager's as well. As the task was not easy for the two, they sometimes needed other managers' help.

Identically ranked employees sometimes performed different tasks. The Senior Salesperson and Management Trainee, who had the same rank, were assigned to different work. While the former was rotated mainly among managerial tasks, the Management Trainee was responsible for the CS checkup and was sometimes assigned to front-line work. The Advanced Salespersons who had worked at different stores before being relocated to the EPC store were assigned to all of the four task categories while Advanced Salespersons who had worked at only one store would seldom be assigned to these.

Full-time Salespersons also differed. While an experienced Full-time Salesperson was responsible for making the layout, another would be assigned to the back room to learn basic inventory control skills. These differences are mainly caused by employees' different level of skills.

Company-Specific Skills

Managerial and front-line work were both based on the company's manuals, which emphasize standardization; the company expected employees to follow the manuals closely and generate profits by achieving high-cost performance. While the company used scientific management, including standard time and standardized procedures, to pursue high job efficiency, Ichi also expected that the pursuit of cleanliness and order on the shop floor would help build a "Japanese-like" image. The brand image was also enhanced through the practice of CS, which I will leave to the chapter on promotion.

The company established standard times for tasks, standard procedures for cashiers and employees in the fitting room, and standardized VMD on the shop floor. Standard time was a basic reference used by full-timers while calculating items such as the labor budget, the work schedule, and employee assignments for the layout.

The company's standard formula for calculating the labor budget was designed to pursue high-cost performance through scientific management by setting a standard time for each kind of work. This was based on the industrial engineering concept of determining standard times and standard requirements (including methods and workflows) with detailed divisions of labor and job descriptions to increase job efficiency (Hales, 1993; Littler, 1982; McAuley et al. 2007: 159). Frederick Taylor points out that industrial engineering was first practiced by Frank Gilbreth, who calculated the necessary time for each task, resulting in higher job efficiency (Taylor, 1903). These ideas echo the founder of Ichi, who strongly believes that job efficiency is crucial. Besides setting the annual labor budget, higher-ranked employees doing this task were also required to set a monthly labor budget to make the daily assignments. Because of its standardization and design roots, the process was not supposed to change randomly.

Cashiers were required to handle a purchase process within 75 seconds, and fitting room employees were expected to serve a customer within one minute. When finding a lineup at the cash registers or outside the fitting room, they were to call for help by walkie-talkie. The founder especially stressed the importance of time-saving strategies in improving customer satisfaction. Salespersons were not expected to fold products slowly but to finish folding within a certain time, such as Full-time Salespersons handling seven T-shirts or Advanced Salespersons eight. There were no time limits for other types of products during my fieldwork; however, the company was highly likely to add standard times soon. Quickness was expected during replenishment. A Full-time Salesperson had to replenish one carbon box within 15 minutes and an Advanced Salesperson within ten minutes. The time limit for one pants alteration was seven minutes (without compromising quality). To go home without leaving any tasks for their colleagues, employees asked the higher-ranked employees to set the target two hours before they finished their work. When the time came, either the employees would ask the higher-ranked employees for the day's goals or the higher-ranked employees would give the goals to the employees.

Besides setting standard times, the company set standard procedures at the two important locations on the shop floor: the cash register and the fitting room. Although the company claimed that these locations helped "soft" processes such as building the store's brand image, their actual intention was more practical. By standardizing procedures, the company achieved high job efficiency and helped it attract employees who performed equally effectively. This standardization left some space for employee creativity, such as in their interactions with customers; however, the company focused more on the standardization of its system.

I shall now describe a case of standard procedure in the fitting room (see Figure 5.2). Employees assigned to the fitting room had four standard steps to follow, as the figure shows. The EPC store allowed customers to try on only three products at once. Thus, employees put the number card and the products into a shopping basket and then showed the customer to the room, leaving the basket with the customer. If the room had a curtain, the employee would close it. If the customer requested alterations, the employee would help

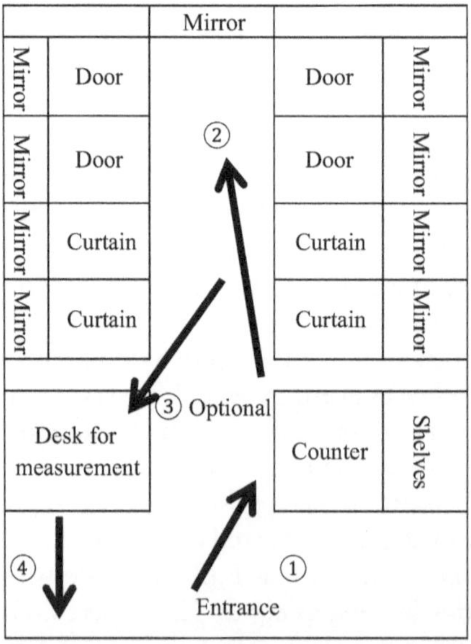

Figure 5.2 Standard procedure at the fitting room, EPC store, 2011, created by the author.

the customer place safety pins to measure the proper length. When the customer came out of the fitting room, the employee would check the number of products again. For those customers who ordered alterations, the employee would measure the length, write a temporary receipt, hand the product to the alteration room, and finally clean the fitting room.

The third practice is the standardization of VMD on the shop floor, intended to build a unified and global image for Ichi, reflecting the founder's view of the necessity of a "Global One" (with emphasis on the "One'). There were several kinds of displays, among which mannequins in show windows were usually regarded as the most important because they were the "face" of the store. Full-body and half-body mannequins were also used. Detailed and strict instructions on full-body mannequins were sent from the Head Office every week (see the black circle in Figure 5.3). The company's Employee Manual contains instructions on the color of various mannequins. Employees were allowed to "decorate" half-body mannequins as they pleased (see the white smile in Figure 5.3) based on the requirements in the Employee Manual.

The company intended to build its brand image through *kijun* (standard) on the shop floor and the practice of CS. The *kijun*, the pursuit of cleanliness and order, was expected to contribute to brand building. There were five ranks, S to D, reflecting cleanliness and order. Cleanliness was an important goal, such as in the fitting room or other locations on the shop floor. Mopping the shop floor and cleaning all the mirrors were examples of maintaining cleanliness. The EPC store had a standard mopping map, but few employees followed it since they cared less about efficiency than about finishing their tasks on time. Order was supposed to be maintained by resolving D-rank situations. Another important factor was that, no matter how eager they might have been to finish their tasks quickly, employees could not forget Ichi's CS policy. Though CS did not appear in work schedules, all employees were expected to practice it.

The practice of CS was controlled by various checkups, including the CS team's, managerial task. Those assigned to the CS team had to be familiar with the requirements on the CS Check Sheet and I will explain in detail about the contents in Chapter 7. The daily CS checkup usually took an hour. After the daily evaluation, they gave the employees feedback. Every month, the Store Manager is supposed to collect the Check Sheet and hold a meeting with employees regarding their CS performance. Because of its linkage with salaries, this practice was designed to encourage employees to practice CS and improve their skills.

The CS requirements actually reduced employee efficiency regarding cleanliness and order since this standardization did not consider the differences in Hong Kong customers' behaviors. Employees understood the store's cleanliness requirements, but so many customers kept asking questions that employees could not finish their work on time. It was not hard to find employees who were "stuck" with a customer in the middle of a cleanliness

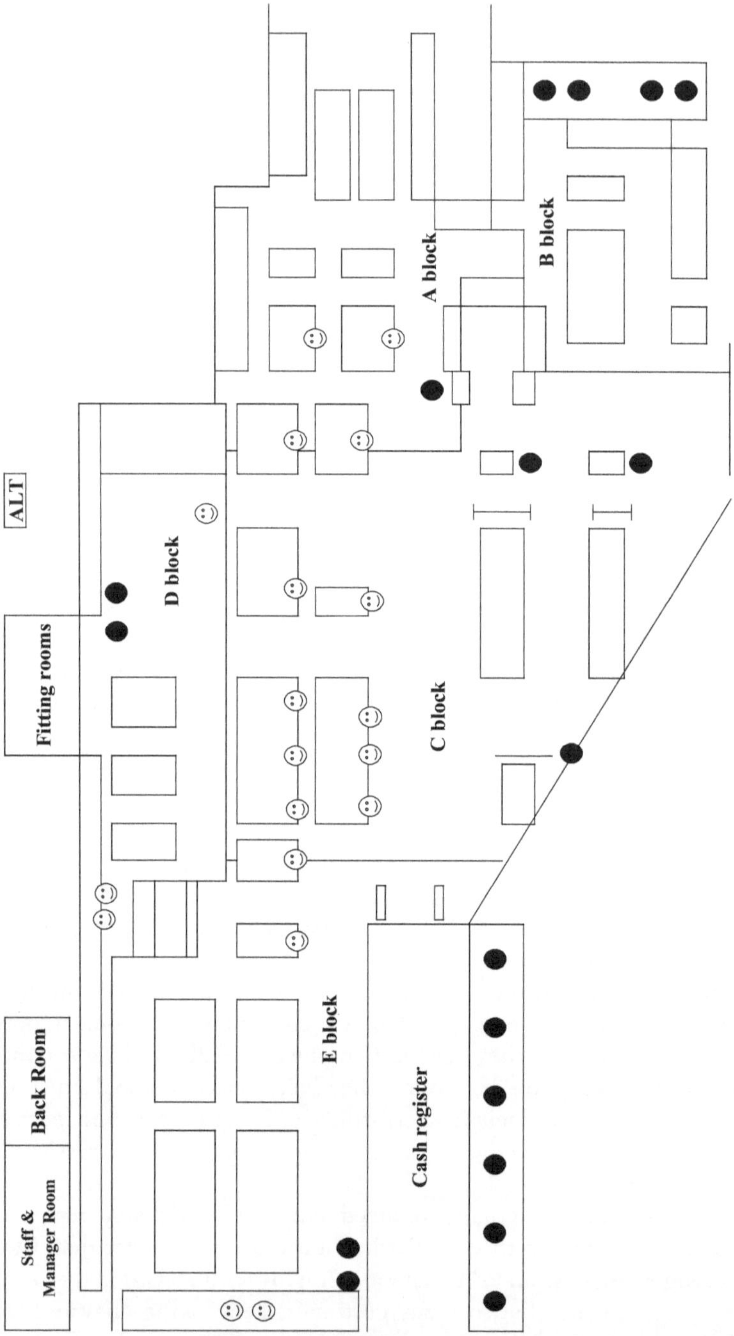

Figure 5.3 Visual merchandising display at the EPC store, 2011, created by the author.

task and thus failed to finish on time. Due to the necessity of cleanliness for brand building, such employees were negatively evaluated even though it was the customers who had slowed them down. Furthermore, the company preferred that customers not open certain packages, such as products for babies, to prevent the entry of harmful bacteria. However, employees found many open packages every day, which required additional time. Customers in Hong Kong liked to try products on or at least unfold the products to check their details. Most then left the products without re-folding them. This practice, perhaps not abnormal in most countries, is rare in Japan. Besides the different shopping customs, the higher brand visibility of Ichi in Japan made customers familiar with the cut and size of Ichi products, giving them less of a need to try them on. The increase in mainland Chinese tourists with different customs might have contributed to these differences. Therefore, employee inefficiency in terms of cleanliness and order was caused by an over-standardization.

Ichi has unique standardizations in its hardware and software. This has somewhat limited the market value of Ichi employees, especially those who have general or meager skills in Hong Kong, where the market tends to prefer specialists able to perform a specific job efficiently. For instance, recruitment advertisements for Western and domestic apparel companies in Hong Kong[1] have stated clearly that employees with specialist knowledge and abilities in a particular area, such as inventory control or cash, are more welcome than those with broad but general knowledge. In recent years, because of the higher sales of Ichi in Hong Kong, the company's employees have become desirable to foreign apparel companies. However, only those ranked above Assistant Store Manager are likely to be headhunted and offered attractive wages. Most such people have worked at Ichi for a relatively long time and have front-line experience than exceeds company-specific knowledge. For instance, a Store Manager who had worked for more than six years at Ichi was headhunted to an American apparel retailer as an area manager while another Assistant Store Manager moved to another American apparel retailer as a senior manager. However, their cases are rare; most employees who were less skilled and had only rote memorization of company-specific knowledge found it hard to change careers and obtain higher pay.

Training "Ichi Man"

The examination above showed that each Ichi task had detailed requirements. As in Japan, Hong Kong's retail industry is highly mobile, posing a tough problem for Ichi. The company attempted to retain skilled employees by training multifunctional workers who could fit into any kind of work, thus guaranteeing immediate replacements. Ichi used two methods to achieve this goal: OJT and egalitarian job rotation.

As the words imply, OJT consisted of training inside the store. Ichi policy made it compulsory. New employees were expected to receive OJT on their first day of work. At the EPC store, this usually lasted for three hours, starting with the introduction of the store layout and the names of all the products, which new employees were expected to remember. Then, they learned how to fold products in each block. They began in A block, where the female items were collected, and learned how to fold T-shirts in the summer and woolen sweaters in the winter. B block was usually skipped at the EPC store, as it had few customers; this was not allowed because new employees became confused later when customers asked them to suggest the proper size or shape. At C block, which mainly featured male items, new employees were taught how to fold shirts, considered a relatively difficult job. They then moved to D block, which housed both female and male jeans and trousers. The method of folding those products was not standardized at the EPC store, so employees usually did not spend much time there. Finally, at E block, a place for kid's items and male accessories, employees learned how to fold tiny products.

The OJT seemed to focus on folding methods. Other necessary issues were not covered, such as how to put disordered items back into a package and the fastest way to convert centimeters into inches. After three hours of training, employees were basically "thrown onto" the shop floor and had to get help from superiors or experienced colleagues. The short OJT obviously did not intend to teach them everything but expected them to get used to the work by themselves. It was very common to find new employees wondering what to do in the first few weeks, especially during the slow season. They just paced up and down near the product shelves since they did not know what kind of work was appropriate to do, although they could ask other experienced employees. It took quite a long time for them to understand how to deal with problems, as more experienced employees usually helped prevent D-rank situations and served customers voluntarily. The worst was in the peak season when new employees could not answer customer questions while other employees were too busy to help.

Although new employees were expected to ask for help, not every experienced colleague was willing to assist because they were busy too. As I was working in D block, which was close to the fitting room, a part-timer who had worked for more than three months hurried out of the fitting room and complained about a new worker:

> You know the new girl here? She is so slow! I asked her to 'RUN' for the fitting room and handed her only three pieces of clothing, but she hasn't come back yet! Can you believe that? Yesterday I worked with her, I know how slow she is, so I reduced the number of clothes this time, and still she was late. She just slows down our job!

It turned out that the new girl did not even know the product shelf and had to search for it piece by piece, which took her a long time. I wondered why the more experienced part-timer did not just tell her the location. The coercive attitudes of some of the experienced employees sometimes made newcomers afraid to ask for help although everyone knew that it was not easy for new employees who had worked for only one or two days a week to master everything at once and appear experienced

Although OJT was considered necessary and compulsory, its effect was questionable since insufficient guidance was given, and new employees had to learn on their own. Some higher-ranked employees did not conduct OJT very seriously because of the high mobility of employees, especially part-timers, while others offered no OJT at all. Not all stores in Ichi Hong Kong provided OJT for numerous reasons, including the labor shortage and insufficient time. To fill this gap, job rotation was developed.

Job rotation was designed to train multifunctional workers through the frequent rotation of job assignments inside the store. Though the company expected job assignments to be carried out based on rank and status, the reality might have been different. A five-day work schedule showing the job rotations of several employees at the EPC store serves as an example (see Table 5.2). Three categories of managerial work and ten of front-line work were shown in the daily work schedule, as seen earlier. While managerial work covered checks and assignments, CS and human resources, the front-line work comprised the cash register, various blocks, the fitting room, "RUN," alteration, replenishment, cleaning, back room, and organizing products.

Because of the limited space of each daily work schedule, the term for every job task was shortened: "CA" for cash register, "FR" for a fitting room, "CHK" for item check, "STI" for pasting stickers, "BR" for the back room, "FR" for a fitting room, "LAY" for layout change, "ALT" for alteration, and "S/S" for organizing products. The blocks were represented by the letters A to E. Meanwhile, "Back" and "Door" were used to indicate the back and front parts of blocks A and C, respectively. The numbers 1 to 4 were used for the cash registers, indicated as "POS1," "POS2," "POS3," and "POS4." Because "POS4" was closest to the entrance, employees were expected to use it at any time, while "POS1" was for those helping when there were too many customers waiting in line or for discounts on purchases of the employer's merchandise. The job indicated by "DUS," short for "DUST," refers to cleaning in the schedules for October 10 and 12 and November 8 but was not shown afterward because, in early October, the Head Office required all employees to take care of their own location before the store opened, thus making this task part of the daily work schedule; after two months, however, this task disappeared from the store's daily work schedule. Break time was shown as '0'. The timing of breaks depended completely on the higher-ranked employees, who made the daily work schedule.

Twelve employees were chosen for the examination of job rotation patterns: three higher-ranked employees (one Senior Salesperson, one Management Trainee, and one Advanced Salesperson), five full-time salespersons, and four part-timers. The number represented the length of work experience: the smaller the number, the longer the work experience at Ichi. Part-timer 1 entered the EPC store earlier than part-timer 2, while part-timer 2 joined

Table 5.2 Job rotation at the EPC store, 2010–2011

Date	Employees	Sex	Before the Opening			During the opening								
			08:00	08:30	09:00	09:30	10:00	10:30	11:00	11:30	12:00	12:30	13:00	13:30
	Senior Sales	M												
	Management Trainee	F												
10 Oct 2010 (Sun)	Advanced Sales	F									POS3	POS3	POS3	POS3
	Full-time Sales 1	M												
	Full-time Sales 2	M		REP	C	REP	C	DUS	C	C	BR	D	BR	D
	Full-time Sales 3	F												
	Part-timer 1	M												
	Part-timer 2	M												

Date	Employees	Sex	Before the Opening			During the opening								
			08:00	08:30	09:00	09:30	10:00	10:30	11:00	11:30	12:00	12:30	13:00	13:30
	Senior Sales	M		CHK	SHEET	CHK	POP	CHK	PR	CHK	PR	CHK	A	CHK
	Management Trainee	F		PR	PR	PR	PR	DUS	C	C	CS	CHK	CA	CHK
	Advanced Sales	F										ALT	POS4	ALT
12 Oct 2010 (Tue)	Full-time Sales 1	M												
	Full-time Sales 2	M		REP	REP	REP	C	DUS	FR	FR	FR	FR	FR	FR
	Full-time Sales 4	F												
	Part-timer 1	F												
	Part-timer 3	M										C	C	C
	Part-timer 4	M		REP	C	REP	D	DUS	B	B	B	B	B	B

Date	Employees	Sex	Before the Opening			During the opening								
			08:00	08:30	09:00	09:30	10:00	10:30	11:00	11:30	12:00	12:30	13:00	13:30
	Management Trainee	F												
8 Nov 2010 (Mon)	Senior Sales	M		DEL	CHK	REP	CHK	REP	人件	CHK	NEW	CHK	NEW	CHK
	Full-time Sales 5	M									FR	FR	FR	FR
	Part-timer 1	M												
	Part-timer 3	M		REP	A	REP	E	DUS	E	E	E	E	0	0
	Part-timer 4	F		REP	B	REP	B	DUS	C	C	O	O	E	E

Date	Employees	Sex	Before the Opening			During the opening								
			08:00	08:30	09:00	09:30	10:00	10:30	11:00	11:30	12:00	12:30	13:00	13:30
	Management Trainee	F		SHEET	POP	CHK	CHK	CHK	C	CHK	ALT	CHK	B	CHK
	Senior Sales	M		CHK	CHK	CHK	CHK	CHK	0	0	HO	HO	HO	HO
1 Dec 2010 (Wed)	Advanced Sales	F												
	Full-time Sales 1	M		REP	REP	REP	REP	DUS	POS4	POS4	POS4	POS4	POS4	POS4
	Full-time Sales 2	M												
	Full-time Sales 5	F												
	Part-timer 1	M												
	Part-timer 2	M												

Date	Employees	Sex	Before the Opening			During the opening								
			08:00	08:30	09:00	09:30	10:00	10:30	11:00	11:30	12:00	12:30	13:00	13:30
	Management Trainee	F												
	Senior Sales	M												
20 Dec 2010 (Mon)	Full-time Sales 4	M	REP	C	REP	C	REP	C	FR	FR	FR	FR	FR	FR
	Full-time Sales 5	M												
	Part-timer 1	M	REP	E	REP	E	REP	E	POS2	POS2	POS2	POS2	E	E
	Part-timer 3	M	REP	D	REP	D	REP	D	A	DOOR	0	0	POS2	POS2
	Part-timer 4	F	REP	E	REP	E	REP	E	POS3	POS3	0	POS3	POS3	POS3

14:00	14:30	15:00	15:30	16:00	16:30	17:00	17:30	18:00	18:30	19:00	19:30	20:00	20:30	21:00	21:30
		E	CHK	LAY	PLAN	CHK	0	0	A	CHK	B	CHK	C	CHK	D
		CS	CHK	CS	0	0	C	CHK	POS4	CHK	POS4	CHK	POS4	CHK	POS4
POS3	POS3	POS3	POS3	0	0	CHK	POS3	POS3	POS3	POS3	POS3	POS3	POS3	POS3	
		POS4	POS4	ALT	C	RUN	RUN	0	0	FR	FR	FR	FR	ALT	S/S
BR	D	0	0	DEL	LAY	MAP									
			FR	FR	FR	FR	FR	FR	FR	0	0	C	C	C	C
		C	C	C	C	C	C	POS2	POS2	0	0	D	D	D	D
		B	B	B	0	0	E	E	E	E	E	E	E	E	E

14:00	14:30	15:00	15:30	16:00	16:30	17:00	17:30	18:00	18:30	19:00	19:30	20:00	20:30	21:00	21:30
B	CHK	0	0	D	CHK	E	CHK								
0	0	C	CHK	CS	FR	FR	FR								
POS4	ALT	POS4	ALT	0	0	A	CHK	B	CHK	C	CHK	D	CHK		
		FR	FR	FR	0	0	POS4	ALT	POS4	ALT	POS4	ALT	POS4	POS4	POS4
FR	FR	0	0	POS4	ALT	POS4									
		MOP	RUN	0	0	BR	POS3	BR	POS3	BR	POS3	BR	POS3	BR	POS3
								RUN	RUN	RUN	0	A	A	A	A
C	C	C	B	B	0	0	A	A	A	A	A	0	C	C	C
B	B	B	0	0	C	C	C								

14:00	14:30	15:00	15:30	16:00	16:30	17:00	17:30	18:00	18:30	19:00	19:30	20:00	20:30	21:00	21:30
		POS4	POS4	POS4	POS4	POS4	POS4	0	0	FR	FR	FR	FR	FR	FR
0	0	CA	CHK	FR	CHK	C	CHK								
FR	FR	FR	FR	0	0	FR	FR	FR	0	BR	D	BR	D	BR	D
		B	B	CA	RUN	CA	RUN	B	B	0	0	MOP	B	B	B
C	C	C	C	C	C	C	C	C	C						
E	E	POS2	RUN	POS2	RUN	D	D	D	D						

14:00	14:30	15:00	15:30	16:00	16:30	17:00	17:30	18:00	18:30	19:00	19:30	20:00	20:30	21:00	21:30
D	CHK	0	0	A	CHK	C	CHK								
HO	HO	HO	HO	HO	HO	HO	HO								
		C	CHK	D	CHK	0	0	B	CHK	D	CHK	C	CHK	ASS	ASS
POS4	POS4	0	0	ALT	ALT	FR	FR	FR	FR						
		C	DOOR	C	DOOR	C	DOOR	0	0	FR	RUN	FR	RUN	BR	BR
		FR	FR	FR	FR	0	0	POS4	POS4	POS4	POS4	POS4	POS4	POS4	POS4
		POS3	E	B	B	B	B	0	0	C	DOOR	C	DOOR	C	DOOR
								C	DOOR	0	A	A	A	A	A

14:00	14:30	15:00	15:30	16:00	16:30	17:00	17:30	18:00	18:30	19:00	19:30	20:00	20:30	21:00	21:30
		人件	CHK	C	CHK	0	0	CHK	B	CHK	C	CHK	D	CHK	E
		BR	BR	0	0	CHK	ASS	CHK	ASS	CHK	ASS	CHK	ASS	CHK	ASS
FR	FR	0	0	BR	BR	C	DOOR	C	DOOR						
		FR	FR	FR	FR	0	0	C	BACK	POS4	POS4	POS4	POS4	POS4	POS4
A	DOOR	0	0	REP	REP	REP	REP								
POS2	POS2	POS2	POS2	POS2	POS2	POS2	POS2								
POS3															

Table 5.2 (Continued)

Date	Employees	Sex	After the opening			
			22:00	22:30	23:00	23:30
10 Oct 2010 (Sun)	Senior Sales	M	ASS	ASS	S/S	CHK
	Management Trainee	F	CU	CU	CU	CU
	Advanced Sales	F				
	Full-time Sales 1	M	ALT	PR	PR	NEW
	Full-time Sales 2	M				
	Full-time Sales 3	F	S/S	C	S/S	C
	Part-timer 1	M	S/S	D	S/S	D
	Part-timer 2	M	S/S	E	S/S	E

Date	Employees	Sex	After the opening			
			22:00	22:30	23:00	23:30
12 Oct 2010 (Tue)	Senior Sales	M				
	Management Trainee	F				
	Advanced Sales	F				
	Full-time Sales 1	M	S/S	CA	S/S	A
	Full-time Sales 2	M				
	Full-time Sales 4	F	S/S	D	S/S	D
	Part-timer 1	F	S/S	A	S/S	A
	Part-timer 3	M	S/S	C	S/S	C
	Part-timer 4	M				

Date	Employees	Sex	After the opening			
			22:00	22:30	23:00	23:30
8 Nov 2010 (Mon)	Management Trainee	F	CU	CU	CU	CU
	Senior Sales	M				
	Full-time Sales 5	M	S/S	BR	D	D
	Part-timer 1	M	S/S	B	B	A
	Part-timer 3	M				
	Part-timer 4	F				

Date	Employees	Sex	After the opening			
			22:00	22:30	23:00	23:30
1 Dec 2010 (Wed)	Management Trainee	F				
	Senior Sales	M				
	Advanced Sales	F	S/S	CHK	S/S	CHK
	Full-time Sales 1	M				
	Full-time Sales 2	M	S/S	BR	S/S	C
	Full-time Sales 5	F	CU	CU	CU	CU
	Part-timer 1	M	S/S	C	C	C
	Part-timer 2	M	S/S	A	A	A

Date	Employees	Sex	After the opening			
			22:00	22:30	23:00	23:30
20 Dec 2010 (Mon)	Management Trainee	F	ASS	ASS	CHK	S/S
	Senior Sales	M	CHK	ASS	S/S	CHK
	Full-time Sales 4	M				
	Full-time Sales 5	M	LAY	OUT	LAY	OUT
	Part-timer 1	M				
	Part-timer 3	M				
	Part-timer 4	F				

A A block
B B block
C C block
D D block
E E block
RUN RUN
LAY Layout
MOP Cleaning
REP Replenishment
CHK Check item
STI Paste stickers
POS Cash Register
S/S Organize products
BACK Back side
Door Near Entrance
FR Fitting Room

earlier than part-timer 3. In October 2010, the Management Trainee and Senior Salesperson were ranked as the same grade; however, the Management Trainee was promoted to Assistant Store Manager in November, so she was put above the Senior Salesperson in the daily work schedule. To prevent confusion, I kept her job title as "Management Trainee." Because of the difficulty of obtaining precise work schedules, the data for some employees are insufficient. I will first examine how the employees were rotated within the specific categories of the higher-ranked managerial and front-line work and then analyze their rotation to determine the relationship between job rotation and the importance of rank.

As the daily work schedule above shows, employees were frequently rotated to different jobs within a single task or among various work categories in order to make them familiar with all store tasks. In fact, the daily work schedule was only a "plan" since employees experienced more than what was written in the schedule. Flexible assignments are more often observed in front-line work because of their overlapping tasks, as has been discussed. Looking at the job rotations of different employee groups, we see that higher-ranked employees were frequently rotated within a single managerial task, checks, and assignments, allowing them to enhance their skills in that task. The Senior Salesperson had to check blocks and sometimes had to check other places as well, like the fitting or alteration room. The Management Trainee was assigned to more than three different jobs within one task. The Advanced Salesperson was less frequently rotated but was also rotated within a single task. Most other managerial tasks, such as CS, were assigned to the CS team. Although higher-ranked employees were never assigned formally to front-line work in the daily work schedule, they often helped with the cash register and customer service when necessary. All EPC Store Managers were given front-line work experience when they started.

Full-time Salespersons were usually rotated within the same or different categories of front-line work. When rotating within the same task on the sales floor, they were assigned to C block, A block, sometimes D block, "RUN," and layout. For instance, on October 10, 2010, Full-time Salesperson 1 worked at C block and was then assigned to "RUN." Full-time Salesperson 2 was also assigned to C block and then to D block and finally to the layout. Full-time Salesperson 3 was assigned only to C block. On December 1, 2010, only Full-time Salesperson 1 was assigned to work at the entrance of C block and to "RUN." On December 20, 2010, Full-time Salesperson 1 was again assigned to work on various sales floor tasks, such as the back of C block and layout. Full-time Salespersons were seldom assigned to do replenishment in the daily work schedules, but they might help when necessary. They even helped to change the mannequins although it was not written on the schedules. Full-time salespersons were also frequently rotated among different categories of work in the Front-line work. Full-time Salesperson 1 worked for three different tasks within one day, first cashier, then alternation, and finally fitting room. Full-time Salesperson 3 worked in the fitting room, cash register, and alternation on 12 October 2010. Full-time Salesperson 2 had a similar experience on 1 December 2010.

Part-timers, who were outside the official hierarchy of the company, were also often rotated among blocks. For instance, part-timer 1 worked in two blocks C and D on 10 October 2010 he then was assigned to A block on 12 October 2010. In the following days, he worked at E and B blocks. Only during a few days, he worked at all blocks. Two other part-timers had the similar path. This showed that even though part-timers might not work for a long time at the store they were 'equally' dealt with in terms of performing multifunctional work. They were even expected to perform some works that were not written in the daily work schedule at all, such as serving customers with product knowledge, taking alternated products, organizing products based on the company's manuals, and so on. On 20 December 2010, three part-timers were all assigned to the cash register to work for more than three hours which made them feel superior to others just because of the importance of the place which could differentiate them from others. Blocks like B and D blocks usually were not so popular because everyone knew that work in those blocks was not only boring but also very hard. In any case, compared with full-timers, the skill formation of part-timers was limited. New part-timers were usually assigned work with the characteristics of high visibility, immobility, minority, and strong requisite of CS, while experienced part-timers were assigned to places with fewer visibilities compared with new part-timers. It was clear for part-timer 1 and part-timer 4 on 12 October. 2010.

The above description shows the picture of how store employees were frequently rotated within the store. There were reasons for the company to put its focus on training multifunctional employees. Firstly, with enough multifunctional employees in the store, it was much easier to adapt to the unexpected situation as the retail industry was greatly influenced by the high mobility of employees, especially in Hong Kong where competition was always severe for qualified people. No one can predict how long full-timers would work for the company, let alone those part-timers. Some employees quitted their job suddenly which usually made higher-ranked employees very hard to find the replacement easily. Sufficient multifunctional workers would help them to prevent such kind of difficulty.

Secondly, multifunctional employees were expected to respond more quickly to various requests from customers who usually considered all employees to know everything in the store and tended to ask any kind of questions. Some customers might ask an employee working in B block to bring certain products from A or C block while others might want an employee in the fitting room to measure sizes for them. It was also very often to hear from customers at the cash register to request suggestions from employees about other products. To handle this kind of problem, multifunctional employees were considered to be more capable than those who just had knowledge about one specific area.

It was common general that while managers were frequently rotated among or within different categories of managerial work, other full-timers and part-timers were rotated in the Front-line work. Although this was not exactly the same to what Koike observed in egalitarian rotation in a Japanese factory (1984), the frequency of their rotation was quite high compared with some Western counterparts. A female Full-time Salesperson at the EPC store who used to work at ZARA claimed that the required works at Ichi were far more than her previous job where she was assigned only to the kid's section but never to other blocks. Different from Ichi, ZARA expected their employees to become specialists rather than multifunctional workers.

Rotation and Career Path

While job rotation between managerial work and front-line work inside one store aims to train additional multifunctional workers to prevent the sudden shortage of efficient labor, inter-store and store-office rotations are also practiced at the EPC store. Such practice has important implications for employees who wish to be promoted. Personnel relocation is conducted in March and September every year. The Human Resources Department announces the personnel relocation issue. The announcement, which is written on a sheet of A4 paper, usually includes the name of the staff to be relocated and the store to which he or she would be relocated to. The announcement is circulated in the related store for reference at the end of either February or August.

The inter-store rotation has three major purposes: internal promotion, personnel adjustment, and opening new stores. The first two types of rotation are regularly practiced in March and September, whereas the last one is performed only when it is necessary. All three types of inter-store rotation require the recommendation of the Store Manager and the approval of superiors. The company discourages self-recommendation. A full-timer is not supposed to be relocated within half a year. This section focuses on two types of inter-store rotation: internal promotion and the opening of new stores, which are more related to workers' future career paths.

Inter-store rotation means an employee would receive an internal promotion because such is regarded as necessary to his/her future career path and is implicitly influenced by informal store ranking. The ideal career path of employees in Ichi is to learn skills from B-rank stores to a B+-store and finally an A-rank store because higher-ranked stores usually require more experience and knowledge. However, this career path is not always followed. A Senior Salesperson at the EPC store was relocated from the Festival Walk store, which is a B+-store, to the B-ranked EPC store. However, the Senior Salesperson was happy with it, saying, "I feel lucky to be relocated to such a small store because there are fewer competitors here, so I have more time to learn new skills and can attempt to jump to an A-rank store."

Inter-store rotation also offered a "free pass" to the promotion of a Store Manager who expected to accumulate experience working at different stores in advance. When the Assistant Store Manager at the EPC store who successively worked at an A- and a B-rank store was promoted to Deputy Store Manager and relocated to an A-rank store, everyone knew that she was on her way to being promoted to Store Manager in the near future. Jenny, the Store Manager at the EPC store whose first store was B-rank, also acquired experience in an A-rank store before the promotion. The Store Manager Lisa, who worked in four different stores, also fit this example. Several would-be Store Managers were also sent only to A-rank stores but never to only B-rank stores. One interesting thing is that the reputation of the Store Manager sometimes plays a significant role in employees' inter-store rotation. Two ex-Full-time Salespersons of the EPC store were promoted because of the good reputation of their Store Manager and the latter's concern and assistance to employees.

The second type of inter-store rotation is implemented when a new store opens and labor force is required. Regardless of the size of the store, employees are generally willing to be relocated to new stores because they believe that they can learn more skills after relocation. This type of rotation is practiced two to three months before opening and involves full-timers, including the Store Manager, and sometimes even part-timers. When the EPC store opened in 2007, Cathy and Oliver, two full-timers, were transferred from the Plaza Hollywood store, which was close to the EPC store. Cathy was transferred after working at Plaza Hollywood for several months because of serious labor shortage at that time. Oliver was selected because the EPC store lacked male employees. When the biggest standard store opened in Hong Kong in November 2010, Helen and Aiki, two full-timers were relocated there from the EPC store. The relocation was unusual because Helen was directly selected by Mizuno, the Operations Manager, rather than the Store Manager. In October 2010, Mizuno was looking for the "best" candidates for the opening of the new store. Mizuno, in a private interview, could not help expressing his favorable impression of Helen; he was very proud of having such an efficient employee.

I: I heard that Helen is going to be relocated.

MIZUNO: That's right. Among all employees that I observed, I found that she, with her strong work enthusiasm, is one of the best. The new store is going to be the largest one in Hong Kong, and it is expected to have high total sales. Because it is the only store to open this year, we will do our best to make it successful. I need to hire the best members from all the stores in Hong Kong, and Helen is just what I want.

While Helen was relocated with the strong support by the Japanese Operations Manager, another Full-time Salesperson, Aiki, was added to the list by the Store Manager of the EPC store, Jenny. Several months after this personnel relocation, Jenny was assigned to open the new store before its opening. As the new Store Manager, she had the authority to select labor force from the EPC store. She selected two part-timers who wanted to become full-timers and two other Full-time Salespersons. When this news was announced, the Full-time Salesperson that was not selected as the relocation candidate was disappointed because he lost a good opportunity for future promotion. Inter-store rotation made everyone realize that the ideal career path for them was to work at different ranked stores within or outside Hong Kong and work for Store Managers with a good reputation and employee-first mindset.

Another major job rotation, store-office relocation is rare in Ichi, Hong Kong; it is conducted mainly among high-ranking managers, university degree holders, or front-line workers fluent in Japanese. Employees who are not qualified are not subjected to this rotation. An Assistant Store Manager who entered the company as a Management Trainee was relocated to the marketing department at the Head Office because of her ability although the real reason for the relocation was that she wanted to have a stable life wherein she would not have to work at midnight. A female employee who worked in the Store Operations Department was relocated from the store to the Head Office. The reason for her relocation was that she is fluent in Japanese; not many employees can speak Japanese fluently in Ichi Hong Kong. A female employee who used to be a Management Trainee at the store was relocated to the Department of Human Resources because of her good educational background in management. Employees who have a university diploma or are fluent in Japanese generally have a better chance of being relocated to the Head Office. Supervisors are sometimes assigned to work at the Head Office. A Japanese Supervisor was relocated to the Department of Store Operations to assist the Japanese Operations Manager. A male local Supervisor was relocated to the department of Ichi University to become the person in charge.

Inter-store rotation is conducted among ordinary employees, whereas store-office rotation is a "privilege" only for a small group of people. Most employees would rather develop a career at the front line than pursue a career at the Head Office. Being relocated to other stores, ideally, after several years of working at the same store and from a B-rank to an A-rank store, is one way to be promoted. However, Ichi discourages self-recommendation; thus, the career paths of employees depend largely on the Store Managers and superiors. For some stores, such as the EPC store, where Supervisors visit less frequently, recommendations and encouragement from Store Managers play a significant role in future promotion.

Conclusion

This chapter revealed the process of skill formation at the EPC store. First, managerial and front-line work were described and defined, and the relation between employees' ranks and their assignment was analyzed. Second, training employees through frequent rotation within one store was examined as well as how inter-store and office-store rotation influences employees' future career paths.

Ambiguous job classification observed in many overlapping work tasks allows the flexible assignment of employees regardless of their formal ranks. An employee can be asked to perform different tasks, and low-ranked employees might be assigned work for high-ranked workers. This vague nature of work prompted the flexible assignment of store employees.

Intra-store rotation contributed largely to creating multifunctional employees for the store as OJT was limited because of insufficient labor. Store employees especially lower-ranked employees were egalitarian and rotated among different tasks of the front-line work. This practice contributed to flexible job assignments and is expected to achieve higher job efficiency. Inter-store rotation was one of the informal premises for the promotion and employees needed to focus on the store skills because of the limited opportunity of the office-store rotation.

The design of the ranking system in Ichi and how it stimulates fast promotion will be discussed in the next chapter. This ranking system encourages employees to develop their skills. The analysis of how the reward system attempts to encourage employees to pursue Ichi-specific skills will likewise be discussed.

Created by the author.

A, A block; B, B block; C, C block; D, D block; E, E block; RUN, RUN; LAY, Layout; MOP, Cleaning; REP, Replenishme; CHK, Check item.

Note

1 Recruitment websites investigated include Career 852, recruit.net, and recruit.com.hk.

References

Aoki, M. (1986) Horizontal vs. Vertical Information Structure of the Firm. *The American Economic Review*, 76(5), pp. 971–983.

Aoki, M. (1990) Toward an Economic Model of the Japanese Firm. *Journal of Economic Literature*, 28(1), pp. 1–27.

Aoki, M. (1992) Decentralization-Centralization in Japanese Organization: A dual Principle. In Kumon, S. and Rosovsky, H. (eds.), *The Japanese Political Economy (Vol. 3)*, pp. 142–169. Stanford, CA: Stanford University Press.

Clark, R. (1979) *The Japanese Company*. Cambridge, MA: Yale University Press.

Hales, C. (1993) *Managing Through Organization*. London: Routledge.

Itoh, H. (1994) Japanese Human Resource Management from the Viewpoint of Incentive Theory. In Aoki, M. and Dore, R. (eds.) *The Japanese Firm: The Sources of Competitive Strength*, pp. 233–264. Oxford: Oxford University Press.

Koike, K. (1984) Skill Formation Systems in the U.S. and Japan: A Comparative Study. In Aoki, M. (ed.), *The Economic Analysis of the Japanese Firm*, pp. 47–75. North Holland: Elsevier Science Publishers B.V.

Littler, C.R. (1982) *The Development of the Labour Process in Capitalist Societies.* London: Heinemann.
McAuley, J., Duberley, J., & Johnson, P. (2007) *Organization Theory: Challenges and Perspectives.* Edinburgh Gate: Pearson Education.
Taylor, F.W. (1903) *Shop Management.* New York: Harper & Bros.
Wong, H.W. (1999) *Japanese Bosses, Chinese Workers: Power and Control in a Hong Kong Megastore.* Richmond, VA: Curzon Press.

6 Monitoring Ideology Dissemination

This chapter examines how the system of ranking and reward is designed to encourage employees to develop their skills further and to become qualified employees. A system of ranking and reward has been standardized in the Hong Kong market, and both Japanese and local employees are under the same system, which is different from what Heung Wah Wong (1999) observed in a Japanese retailer in Hong Kong in the 1990s when he found that a dual-ranking system between Japanese expatriates and local employees exists; in this system, the former is superior to the latter.

This chapter particularly points out that how Ichi uses its corporate system not only to encourage skill development but also to allow the company to "monitor" the progress of the introduction of Ichi DNA in stores.

Ranking System

Employees' ranks comprise five levels from the bottom to top: F, J, S, M, and E ranks, and each rank has a three-month probation period (see Table 6.1). Each rank is divided into three to five ranks. University graduates who were recruited as office employees and as Management Trainees started their career in J3. Some rankings are only for the mid-careers, such as J1, S1, and M1.

The aforementioned information has several implications, which echo the arguments of Wong (1999) and Masahiko Aoki (1992). First, each staff is placed in a standardized frame of ranking because no distinction in ranking is observed between store employees and office employees. Although the starting point of university graduates differs from non-university graduates, all employees are able to compare their rankings with others to confirm their status. Wong (1999: 99) suggests that rank is a social desire for both Japanese and local employees because ranking decides their authority and status within the company. These arguments echo those of Aoki (1992: 147–153) who concluded that Japanese firms have a rank hierarchy, whereas their West counterpart has a functional hierarchy. Wong (1999: 98) echoed his idea and claim that although the Japanese megastore he investigated was hierarchical, rank hierarchy was not functional. The conventional literature claim that the Japanese employment system, which is simply based on seniority, oversimplifies the actual practice.

DOI: 10.4324/9781003305675-6

Table 6.1 Ranking system of full-timers, Ichi Hong Kong, 2011

Level	*Rank*
Executive	E1
	E2
	E3
Leader/director	M1
	M2
	M3
Store Manager/supervisor	S1
	S2
	S3
	S4
	S5
Managers	J1
	J2
	J3
Staff	F1
	F2
	F3

Created by the author.

Second, the company encourages internal promotion rather than direct recruitment of mid-careers from outside because the latter requires time for learning company-specific skills as well as understanding and practicing the *shahū* (company's culture). When the company entered the Hong Kong market in 2005, many mid-careers were recruited both in the office and in stores. Along with the maturity of the market, local subsidiaries expected employees to begin from the bottom of the hierarchy; this practice supports the studies conducted by Aoki (1990), Clark (1979), and Wong (1999). Internal promotion did not only allow the company to gain employees who understood its principles but also workers who could work based on the company's manuals.

Third, the competition is fierce in Ichi, which is similar to the case of what Wong (1999: 100) referred to as "*shusse kyōsō*" (competition to promotion). This competition is a result of the two aforementioned characteristics. Each staff is ranked in the same system regardless of the nature of their jobs; therefore, rank rather than work assignment is the social desire. Moreover, the internal promotion allows employees to compete with their colleagues, which stimulates them to learn more skills.

Examination of functional job titles proves the distinctive feature of Ichi's ranks, which distinguish the company from Japanese companies in early literature. Functional job titles are divided into store operation and office operation, and employees who begin their career in the store can opt for future development in the office from S4 (see Table 6.2).

Employees in the F rank include Full-time (F1), Advanced (F2), and Senior Salespersons (F3) are the main labor force at the stores in Hong Kong. For example, the East Point City (EPC) store had five Full-time, four Advanced,

Table 6.2 Rank and functional title in Ichi Hong Kong, 2011

Rank		*Functional title*	
		Store operation	*Office operation*
E			Executives
M	M3	Franchise owner	Director
	M2		PIC of overseas operation
	M1		Mid-careers
S	S5	Superstar Store Manager	Supervisor
	S4	Star store manager	Block leader
	S3	Store Manager	
	S2	Store Manager	
	S1	Mid-careers, demotion	
J	J3	Deputy store manager	
	J2	Assistant store manager	
	J1	Mid-careers	
F	F3	Senior salesperson/ management trainee	
	F2	Advanced salesperson	
	F1	Full-time salesperson	

Created by the author.

and one Senior Salesperson at that time.[1] Full-time Salespersons (F1) were expected to master the basic skills of store management. Advanced Salespersons (F2) trained subordinates and were sometimes assigned to do front-line work although not as often as Full-time Salespersons. Senior Salespersons (F3) were expected to have excellent skills in managerial and front-line work and were regarded as junior managers. Management Trainees with university diplomas had a similar rank as Senior Salesperson (F3) during the three-month probation period.

The J rank includes mid-careers (J1) who were not promoted but recruited directly from outside, the Assistant Store Manager (J2), and the Deputy Store Manager (J3). The EPC store comprises one Assistant and one Deputy Store Manager and no mid-careers. After probation, Management Trainees are automatically promoted to the position of Assistant Store Manager, whereas Senior Salespersons have to be selected as promotional candidates first and should pass the examination to be promoted to J2. Usually, one to two Management Trainees are available in one store.[2]

S rank is related to both store and office operations. Store operation comprises mid-careers (S1), Store Manager (S2), and Store Manager (S3). Among the 16 stores in Hong Kong, 15 had local Store Managers (S2) although two of them were ranked as S3 by the end of 2011. Similar to mid-careers (J1), not many mid-careers (S1) are employed in Hong Kong because S1 is usually a demotion from S2; such demotion happens frequently in Japan but rarely in Hong Kong.[3] Although Store Manager (S2) and Store Manager (S3) have the same functional title, S2 is regarded as junior Store Manager in Hong Kong, and S3 has more experience than S2. Different from S1, S2, and S3, S4 and S5 belong either to the operations of stores or to the Head Office. When employees are ranked as S3, they can opt to become either a Star Store Manager (S4) in-store operation or a Supervisor (S4) in office operation. The highest rank achieved by local Hong Kong employees was S4, four Star Store Managers (two Japanese and two locals), and four supervisors (two Japanese and two locals) who managed four to six stores by the end of 2012. The major distinction between them was that while the Star Store Manager worked at specific stores to interact more with daily store operations, the Supervisor had to take care of six stores and belonged to the Head Office operation. The same applies to S5, Super Star Store Manager in-store operation, and block leader in the office. The difference between these two is the number of employees and the store they manage. The block leader focuses on the operations of around 50 stores and not on a single-store operation and is more engaged with jobs in the office and the entire block. Super Star Store Managers work for daily store operations at specific stores. Considering the limited market in Hong Kong, no employee is assigned to these two positions.

M rank has three levels: franchise owners in-store operation, the person in charge (PIC) of overseas operation, and directors of the department in office. Ichi Hong Kong has one Japanese department director and two local directors who are ranked as M rank at the Head Office. The highest E rank refers to executives; for example, the CEO of the Hong Kong region is ranked as E.

The first feature of Ichi's functional job titles is that the promotion to the position of Store Manager (S2) was a privilege for university graduates. This attracted many local university graduates in Hong Kong. The second distinctive feature of Ichi's functional job title is its intention to encourage employees to pursue future career paths at the stores. Seven ranks are provided to Store Managers and Store Manager candidates. Ranks of Store Managers are gradually added to the company's hierarchy in an attempt to strengthen the support for store management as part of company reform starting from 1998 when the company in Japan suffered from lower profit. In addition to setting up block leaders (S5) and supervisors (S4) who were expected to support the operation of Store Managers in 1998, the company added the rank of Super Star Store Manager (S5) in 1999. Ichi claims that this practice intended to enhance decentralization in the stores so that Store Managers could communicate easier with the Head Office regarding data collected on-site as well as offer a reliable source for production.

However, such implementation has not achieved what the company expected because of two possible factors. In Hong Kong, most new employees are Full-time Salespersons rather than university graduates. The case in Ichi, Japan, where the number of Management Trainees is higher than that of non-university graduates is different. Given the company-specific knowledge, even though some employees had industrial knowledge, they were not able to start their career from the middle but from the folding products as part-timers. This factor influenced their work incentive as many of these employees believed that their skills deserved a higher rank.

The second factor is that the ambiguous career path after being the Store Manager lowers worker motivation. Although the company expects local employees to fight for the position of Store Manager rather than office work, no local store employees are ranked above Super Star Store Manager (S5) in Hong Kong. The highest-ranked store employees are S4, and most of them had worked for more than seven years at the company, which is not "fast" from the local people's point of view. Therefore, many employees, especially non-university graduates, realized that the road toward being a Store Manager is long, which is contradictory to what the company claimed.

Reward System

The reward system in Ichi, including material and nonmaterial, was designed to encourage employees to develop their Ichi-specific skills. The material reward is the monetary reflection of ranking because the more skills employees learn, the more they earn. Nonmaterial reward aims to encourage the employees spiritually to further learn Ichi-specific skills.

Material Reward

Material rewards for Hong Kong employees in Ichi are of three types: basic salary, bonus, and allowance. Overtime pay is also counted for employees ranked below Store Manager. Moreover, no transportation fee is allocated for employees in Ichi, Hong Kong. The basic salary usually reflects the link with the ranking system. Bonus depends on superior evaluation during grade assessments. Allowance is different between Japanese and local employees, and this book intends to avoid the ethnocentric factor but rather attempts to interpret it from market aspects.

Basic Salary

The basic salary of local employees in Ichi is based on their ranks, meaning their salary is irrelevant to their assignments. The great difference among different ranks indicates the difference in the levels of Ichi-specific skills. For ranks below Deputy Store Manager, salary increases a certain amount for each rank. Even though the Deputy Store Manager and the Store Manager (S2) perform almost the same job, their salary differs significantly. Store Manager (S3) receives more than S2 although their jobs are similar, which means that even though J3 performs the same job as S3, their salary differs greatly. The difference between J3 and S2 and between S3 and S4 is large. The amount of basic salary for full-timers increased by 50% and for part-timers increased by 10%.

Ichi's salary for high ranks in Hong Kong had less competitive edge compared with the industry average or sometimes that of foreign apparel counterparts. In terms of the overall average of the retail industry, the salary for Full-time Salespersons was around the average and did not have much difference compared with other foreign companies although it might be a little higher in some cases. However, the industry range for Store Managers was higher than the salary in Ichi. According to the data provided by one of the informants, the salary of Store Managers in Ichi is lower than that in Forever 21, where the salary of a Store Manager was 130% to 150% higher than that in Ichi in 2011. Indeed, the size of the store and the monthly sales were different between Ichi and other large apparel stores; however, local employees considered the salary in Ichi lower as the job title was the same.

Poor satisfaction with salary has always been a problem in Ichi stores. When some Store Managers in Ichi moved to other foreign apparel retailers, many employees did the same. Although several scholars suggest that the meaning of work content is more important than monetary reward (Takahashi, 2010), the tie between job satisfaction and income is strong.

Several studies suggest that Hong Kong people pursue money aggressively and concluded that local people are groups of people with a profit-seeking mindset (Wong, 1999; Yu, 2012). Fieldwork in the present study indicates that many local employees are quite sensitive to the subject of salary in other apparel companies or retailers. For instance, a female full-timer knew of the wide range of salaries in various retail sectors, such as sales associates at a cosmetic counter or in another Japanese fashion shop. Considering the fluid information on the Web or among local people, the issue of salary is always a challenge for Ichi. Moreover, along with the increase in property and prices of commodities, salary has become a very crucial issue for employees.

Bonus

The close relations between work evaluation and the amount of bonus were designed to encourage employees to learn the company's skills and practice them on the shop floor. A bonus is for full-timers and part-timers. Similar to the situation in Japan, full-timers are able to receive a bonus worthy of a month's salary at least once a year; therefore, the amount of bonus varies according to the ranks of employees and their work performance. If a high sales volume is achieved, ordinary employees could receive a bonus twice a year the amount of which is normally worth a half month's salary; the Store Managers (S2 and S3) could receive a double bonus, which means that they could receive a bonus three times a year.

The amount of the bonus is strictly related to daily performance based on various check sheets. The more workers meet the company's requirements, the higher the possibility of them earning more. The evaluation results are ranked from S to D, five in total, and each level has a different bonus. If an employee's evaluation is of S-rank, he or she could receive a bonus worthy of three months' salary. For instance, if a Store Manager ranked in S2 or S3 was evaluated as S rank in the checkup, she/he could receive a bonus worthy of six months' salary that year. By February 2013, A-rank was worthy of two months and a half salary, B-rank was two months, C-rank was one month and a half, and D-rank was worthy of one month's salary.

Given the strong bonus incentive, a conflict might arise when the Store Manager finds the assessment unfair. The bonus actually works as one of the important incentives for local Store Managers who agree that although the base salary is lower than the average, if they could obtain a higher evaluation, the total amount of salary would not be too bad. Therefore, a conflict with evaluators will arise when the Store Manager feels that the evaluation is unfair. One local Store Manager confronted a Japanese Supervisor who gave her a C-grade on her evaluation. The Store Manager criticized the Supervisor's failure to give her a fair grade by contesting the contents of the evaluation sheet. However, the Supervisor dismissed her claims but left her crying. In the end, the grade did not change and she submitted her resignation that day.

Several policies are provided to encourage part-timers to improve their practices in customer service (CS) and work in the peak seasons by offering extra hourly salaries and additional bonuses. In March 2011, Ichi Hong Kong began to introduce a bonus system called "Good Performance" for both full-timers and part-timers. The assessment largely depends on the result of employees' monthly check sheet for the practice of CS. Full-timers and part-timers who are successfully nominated would receive a certain amount of bonus for that month. One part-timer commented that the bonus is not only extra but also means a lot. The procedure involves two steps. During the first week, the higher-ranked employees responsible for the practice of customer service at the store would evaluate employees and give them points on their CS Check Sheet. In the second week, if the points of employees are above average, higher-ranked employees would recommend them to the Store Manager as "Good Performance" candidates. While higher-ranked employees evaluate their subordinates based on the CS Check Sheet, the latter needs to evaluate themselves on the same sheet to make the result fair and objective.

A peak-season bonus was provided in November 2010. During that time, part-timers were awarded different amount of bonuses based on their work hours. However, filing of sick leave or being late for work would mean forfeiture of receiving this bonus. Although part-timers can apply for different working shifts during the peak season, the final schedule depends on the higher-ranked employees.

Employee performance evaluations, although designed to be objective, differ according to various Store Managers. Although the bonus can motivate employee's performance, this motivation is lost once the employee finds out that the evaluation is unfair and in favor of the Store Manager. In the EPC store, when good performance was practiced in the first month, many part-timers were motivated; several of them attempted to improve their work performance dramatically to obtain a considerable bonus. However, after the first monthly performance evaluation results came out, many of these employees were disappointed as most of the receivers had been working in the store for a long time and were "friends" with the Store Manager. The main reason for dissatisfaction was the ambiguous written and unwritten criteria without a checkup from the third party.

Allowances

Allowance differs not only between full-timers and part-timers but also among part-timers. Part-timers have accident compensation insurance and staff discount but not medical insurance. Local full-timers are entitled to medical insurance and staff discounts but not housing allowances. However, both do not receive the transportation or education support that Japanese Ichi employees enjoy in Hong Kong. Although full-timers and part-timers have staff discounts, the quota for Store Managers and other employees is the same, which was around HK$2,000 during my fieldwork. However, the amount for Japanese Store Managers in Hong Kong is unlimited, which is similar to the situation in Japan. While Japanese Store Managers receive housing allowances, local employees have to put up with ridiculously high rent. Housing allowance is pointed out in this study because in the retail industry, receiving such a high amount of allowance is uncommon for Store Managers.

In addition to housing, the second highest expenditure for local employees is transportation fee. Unlike the present situation in Ichi Japan, Hong Kong employees are often required to work overtime, especially during peak seasons. Occasionally, Hong Kong employees have to work before and after the service hour of public transportation, prompting them to take a taxi even if they live far from the store. Japanese Store Managers receive transportation fee during their first two-month stay in Hong Kong; afterward, they are treated the same as Hong Kong employees. Education support is also offered to Japanese Store Managers to the envy of local employees. A Japanese Store Manager was even able to send his daughter to the local international kindergarten at the company's expense, something that local Store Managers could hardly afford.

The reason Ichi spent large amounts of money on Japanese expatriates while spending so little on local store employees can be interpreted by market incentives rather than simply deemed as ethnocentric. First, the special environment in Hong Kong allows the subsidiary to neglect the needs of local employees. The subsidiary has a certain degree of autonomy on the issue of cost management; however, as a company, the first concern of top management is cost performance and the ambiguous local law that allows the company to have certain discretion. With the increase in rent in Hong Kong and the labor budget, the subsidiary attempts to save "unnecessary" money. One of the local directors in the Head Office said that it is quite good for local full-timers in Ichi because the company pays them overtime salary. For the top management, or more accurately, for employees in the Head Office, their major role is to control the expense. As long as there is no strong resistance, they are reluctant to do any "adjustment." This is based more on the economical reason rather than the ethical issue.

Second, monetary reward is not only important for Japanese employees but also for the company to keep them. A rich allowance is an efficient method of keeping employees within the company and persuading them to relocate anywhere the company wants them to considering that many Japanese are reluctant to go abroad nowadays. A Japanese Store Manager said that he was quite satisfied with the salary and allowance in Ichi because the amount was really good; thus, he was not open to changing jobs.

Nonmaterial Reward

Except for the above material reward, there are three sets of nonmaterial rewards, including a "Photo Contest," "CS award," and "Thank You Card," which were designed to encourage employees to further learn the Ichi DNA manuals in terms of the *kijun* (standard) and the practice of CS. The focus is on the examination of how the company places emphasis on *form* rather than the *heart*. The company's manual is described as a *form* because its contents are standardized so that employees are required to follow them, which means that no flexibility or localization is required in this sense, or more importantly, the customer is prioritized from the *heart*.

The monthly "Photo Contest" is a representative example to show the company's effort to standardize *kijun* of the store, including both the shop floor and the back side, by stimulating competition among different stores. Higher-ranked employees at the store took pictures before the opening and after the closure of the store to compete for the best, or more accurately, most standardized, the outlook of the store. This practice was introduced into the Hong Kong market because it gained a positive effect in Japan as a part of "Best Practices." After pictures were sent to the Head Office, employees at the Department of Store Operation provided feedback to each store by pointing out the weakness and the places that require improvement. The evaluation was completely based on the company's manuals and criteria, including the order of color and size, the volume of the products, floor layout, and so on. The monthly winner receives a prize and gifts, including an award certificate and a trophy.

The Head Office focuses more on the *form* or the appearance of the store through photos without spending time considering other possibilities, such as when a staff places a particular product in a specific location to attract customers or when a disordered shop floor might reflect short labor. The company used a "Photo Contest" as a time-saving method to evaluate whether the store follows the standardized manuals to increase the speed of standardization in the market. The company's manuals are supposed to create a comfortable shopping environment for customers and achieve a high-cost performance.

Adhering to the manuals is the goal of store employees; however, the original intention of Ichi is lost. From the end of 2010 to 2011 in Ichi Hong Kong, the Lee Theater store always won the competition. Many local employees in Hong Kong claim that the major reason for Lee Theater's dominance is the existence of specialists who have high skills in folding products. As one of the full-timers in the Lee Theater store commented, there are "special" employees who can fold products in A-rank. The disadvantage is that because they have to finish the task within time, they are reluctant to help customers and want to "get rid" of customers as soon as possible, which often results in customer complaints. Various other incentives result in such behavior; however, we cannot neglect the significant role of the Store Manager at the Lee Theater who was well known as a person who could earn high evaluations because he knew how to meet the requirements of Ichi.

Similar to the case of the "Photo Contest," the CS award ceremony was a way for the company to promote the practice of standardization and was expected to spiritually praise and encourage employees. The CS award was designed to emphasize recipients' consciousness of *sossen suihan*, which means to become a role model and motivate other store employees. However, an examination of the case of employees at the EPC store indicates that the ambiguity of the selection criteria and the influence of personal attachment between the evaluators and employees cause poor employee satisfaction, which results in employees' lower motivation toward the award.

The CS award ceremony is generally held during the monthly meeting of the Store Manager at the Head Office in Tsim Sha Tsui. This setting intends to allow employees to show their high ability of CS not only to Store Managers in other stores but also to top higher-ranked employees in the Head Office, including the CEO of the Hong Kong region. The Store Managers who have no recipient that month are expected to reflect on their stores and improve the practice of CS.

I would like to share the event of the award ceremony that I participated in on December 8, 2010, with the Store Manager of the EPC store and the award recipient. The ceremony started at 9:30 am at the Head Office of Ichi Hong Kong. While the Store Managers or representatives and top higher-ranked employees of the Hong Kong subsidiary sat in the front rows, the three recipients were asked to sit in the back rows together. After a 30 minutes introduction of the previous month's general situation in terms of sales, the CEO of the Hong Kong region gave a speech for another 30 minutes. The ceremony started around 10:30 am. The CEO of the region stood in front, and every recipient came forward to receive the awards from him. The awards included three gifts: a CS pin, a coupon (around HK$200), and an award certificate. After receiving the awards, everyone offered a short speech on how they felt about the award. The contents of the speech were the same every time, such as "it is an honor to receive such an award" and "it encourages me to further develop my CS skills."

One recipient from the EPC store that month said to me after the ceremony,

> I didn't want this so-called CS pin. It gives me so much pressure because I have to work so hard on this issue from now on. Moreover, I believe

> Chorus (another Full-time Salesperson) was also qualified. I have no idea why I received the award this time.

Referring to his talk, two issues can be discussed here. First, he felt the responsibility as a recipient, which shows that the company's intention worked. Second, the selection of the recipient was ambiguous. Chorus was also highly evaluated by the Store Manager at that time; however, he was not nominated. Chorus said that although he was dissatisfied, he assumed that exhibiting a hostile attitude toward the Supervisor influenced his evaluation result. Every time the Supervisor visited the store, Chorus never voluntarily approached him. He said he disliked the Supervisor who barely visited or supported the store. Moreover, he intentionally did not show up when the Supervisor organized a store meeting. The Store Manager repeatedly told him to be "nice" to the Supervisor. The attitude of the Chorus was "well acknowledged" by the Supervisor.

As the EPC case implies, the selection procedure and criteria of the award recipient are ambiguous because they are not only based on the company's manuals but on personal relations. This, to some extent, negatively influences the motivation of employees. The practice of CS by Chorus was highly evaluated by store employees; however, he was not nominated because of personal reasons. The case of Chorus implicitly gave hints to other store employees that the evaluation was not objective or rational but might be largely determined by the personal preference of the evaluator. This inequality mainly resulted from and was reinforced by the decentralization of power to the Store Manager, who was largely influenced by the Supervisor.

The "Thank You Card" campaign allows employees to share their feelings. Employees are encouraged by the warm words of their colleagues; however, the *form* of practice is more emphasized than employees' actual *feelings*. This campaign was introduced to all stores in Hong Kong at the end of 2010 as a part of "Good Performance" to encourage colleagues and strengthen the collective spirit through writing cards. According to a Japanese Store Manager, this practice was borrowed from the famous practice in Ritz Carlton. Based on the "Global One" policy, this practice was expanded into every market Ichi entered. The "Thank You Card" was a square piece of paper with various designs adopted from the advertisement graphic of the company. The Head Office would regularly deliver a certain number of cards to the store. The design of the card differs every month. If the store is out of cards, they usually use ordinary paper and cut it into the appropriate square size. One side of the card is printed with Ichi's graphic, and the other side is designed for employees to write "thank you" or other comments as long as they encourage colleagues and strengthen human relations. Many store employees in Hong Kong place their written cards on the locker of colleagues. Some stores even have a special board in the staff room for sticking such cards. The actual implementation of this campaign depends on the individual Store Manager; thus, there are different ways of using these cards. Sometimes, the

Head Office sends a "Thank You Card" to a specific store to show the model of the practice.

Ichi focuses more on whether employees actually implement this practice rather than on the effect of this practice or if employees implement the practice by *heart*. When the Japanese Operations Manager and the Supervisor came to the EPC store in the middle of 2010, they asked the Store Manager to put the board full of cards in a more visible place, such as the back of the door. They cared less if the store employees actually meant something on the cards but focused more on if the practice is implemented. Therefore, store employees especially higher-ranked employees regard this campaign as "homework" that they have to "show" to their superiors. Higher-ranked employees often write cards in the staff room during their break time or after work not because they want to thank employees but rather to comply with the order from the Store Manager. One day, I found a card written "thank you for teaching us Putonghua[4]" from the Store Manager. The card surprised me because I knew many local employees dislike Putonghua (or its represented ideology). Clearly, the Store Manager only wrote the card to comply with store requirements and not to me. Considering that I have a poor grasp of Cantonese, trying to speak less while in the store became a practice. Therefore, the Store Manager had nothing to particularly praise me for but had to think of "something." This assumption was soon proven by the Advanced Salesperson who commented that the Store Manager and she finished their "homework" yesterday after work. When asked what she wrote in those cards, she said that she thanked employees for the cakes they brought to work or the drinks they bought. A Full-time Salesperson heard this conversation and showed his sympathy for the Advanced Salesperson. In addition, the second Store Manager I worked with at the EPC store had not written cards in six months.

Conclusion

This chapter provides an analysis of how the company encouraged employees to learn skills through the system of ranking and reward. In the ranking system, most features of Ichi were similar to the early literature written by Aoki (1992), Clark (1979), and Wong (1999) in terms of the same ranking reference for any staff, internal promotion, and fierce competition. The distinctive feature of Ichi was that the company attempted to attract future employees, particularly university graduates, with its "fast" promotion to Store Manager. This "over-standardized" system neglected the fact that most full-time employees in Hong Kong started their careers from the bottom of the hierarchy; thus, that this system is ironically "slow" for them. This disadvantage was reinforced by the practice of internal promotion and the company's specific skills considering that the employees' previous experiences in general were not deemed important.

The material reward was a monetary reflection of the rankings as employees' income is directly linked to their level and extent of Ichi skills. Moreover, employees personally depended on their superiors who determined the amount of their bonuses. Therefore, employees were not only encouraged to develop company-specific skills but also to "show" their progress to their superiors. The nonmaterial reward was designed to encourage employees to learn more skills while being an efficient way for the Head Office to evaluate "objectively" if store employees mastered Ichi skills based on their "superficial" performance rather than checking the details.

The next chapter will examine how the formal system of promotion was designed and how the nature of the promotion system formed the employees' different "presentations."

Notes

1 The number of Full-time Salespersons increased from 2011 because of the introduction of a new policy that encouraged stores to change the labor structure from a part-timer-dominated model to a full-timer one.
2 After March 2011, Management Trainees were assigned to work only with local and experienced high-ranked Store Managers.
3 There was a female Store Manager (S2) who voluntarily applied for S1 because she became pregnant and could not perform as S2.
4 Putonghua means Standard Chinese.

Reference List

Aoki, M. (1990) Toward an Economic Model of the Japanese Firm. *Journal of Economic Literature*, 28(1), pp. 1–27.

Aoki, M. (1992) Decentralization-Centralization in Japanese Organization: A Dual Principle. In Kumon, S and Rosovsky, H. (eds.), *The Japanese Political Economy (Vol. 3)*, pp. 142–169. Stanford, CA: Stanford University Press.

Clark, R. (1979) *The Japanese Company*. Cambridge, MA: Yale University Press.

Takahashi, N. (2010) *Kyomō no seikashugi: nihongata nenkōsei hukkatsu no susume* [*Unrealistic Merit System: Revival of Japanese Seniority-Based System*]. Tokyo: Tsukuma Shobō.

Wong, H.W. (1999) *Japanese Bosses, Chinese Workers: Power and Control in a Hong Kong Megastore*. Richmond, VA: Curzon Press.

Yu, J. (2012) 'Hong Kong Still No.1 for Mainland Chinese Tourists' *South China Morning Post*, 13 November, 2012. Available at: http://www.scmp.com/news/hong-kong/article/1081729/hk-still-no-1-mainland-tourists (retrieved 24 June, 2013).

7 Promotional Activities and a Collective Presentation of the Self

Chapter 6 examined how the company's system of ranking and reward aimed to encourage employees to learn Ichi-specific skills and how the company monitored their skill formation through its corporate system. This chapter discusses the nature of the promotion system and how employees react toward the formal system. The distinctive feature of the promotional criteria was explored in terms of its "real" intention. This chapter also provides an analysis of how employees behave on site for the promotion and how employees manipulate their work performance to achieve their goals.

Formal Promotion System

Figure 7.1 shows the career step of Ichi's formal store employees. Employees who were ranked lower than the Assistant Store Manager had four times a year for the promotion while above-ranked employees had two times per year. Store Managers (S3) could choose their career path to the store operation or office operation. Considering the limited data from higher-ranked employees, the promotional system of store employees was analyzed from Full-time Salesperson to the Star Store Manager.

Generally, three steps for the promotion were observed: recommendation from superiors, written examination, and interview. After employees gained recommendations and approval from their superiors, they took the written examination which varied according to their ranks. The final step was a series of interviews with the Head Office employees or with the participation of the CEO of Ichi Hong Kong for higher-ranked employees.

Superior Recommendation and Approval

Two major check sheets for the assessment of Ichi employees were presented: "Operations Evaluation Check Sheet" and "customer service (CS) Check Sheet." By contrast, the former focused on the general practical skills of employees, whereas the latter focused on their level of CS. Both check sheets had internal and external evaluators.

DOI: 10.4324/9781003305675-7

Rank	Store operation	Examination	Office operation
S4	Star Store Manager	→	S4: Supervisor
	↑		
S3	Store Manager	2 times a year	
	↑		
S2	Store Manager	2 times a year	
S1	↑ Mid-careers Demotion		
J3	Deputy Store Manager	2 times a year	
	↑		
J2	Assistant Store Manager	2 times a year	
J1	↑ Mid-careers Demotion		
F3	Senior Salesperson / Management Trainee	4 times a year	
	↑		
F2	Advanced Salesperson	4 times a year	
	↑		
F1	Full-time Salesperson	4 times a year	

Figure 7.1 Career path for store employees in Ichi Hong Kong, 2011, created by the author.

This check sheet included seven parts: customer service, training subordinates, sales floor, sales plan, work schedule, management, and cost control. Data are based on the check sheets in March 2011 including those for Full-time Salesperson, Advanced Salesperson, Senior Salesperson, Assistant Store Manager, Deputy Store Manager, and Store Manager were provided. Store Manager (S2 and S3) shared the same check sheet with Star Store Manager (S4). In every part of the check sheet, a reference page number in the company's Employee Manual would be listed where the objectives of those practices were described in detail. Each part had a detailed requirement and every requirement is worth two to three points. The rank was determined by either "definitely practiced (○)" or "needs improvement (×)". A check sheet for every rank of the staff was evaluated on a 100-point scale. Full-time Salespersons and Advanced Salespersons had to acquire at least 80 points. The required points were reduced to 70 for employees from Senior Salespersons to Store Managers (S2). In addition, the required point has increased to 75 points for Store Managers (S3).

The major characteristic of this Check Sheet was that while subordinates largely depended on their superiors in terms of the on-the-job training (OJT), superiors had to rely on the performance of subordinates. Take the layout floor making, for example, to see how employees needed help from their superiors to acquire new skills. Full-time Salespersons made the layout through collaboration with direct superiors. When they were promoted to Senior Salespersons, they could make the layout themselves with the approval of the Store Manager. Deputy Store Manager could independently decide the final layout plan without the Store Manager's intervention. This increase in the degree of skills indicated that higher-ranked employees had higher levels of skills and had more knowledge of the whole store operation, which allowed them to work more independently.

For superiors, their promotion was largely influenced by the work performance of subordinates. In terms of the points of each content, parts of "customer service" and "training subordinates," played a significant role in the promotion which comprised more than half of the total points of the check sheet. Reliance on subordinates has increased along with their ranks. While check sheets of Full-time Salesperson and Advanced Salesperson focused more on their self-development in terms of mastering new skills, those employees who were ranked above Senior Salesperson were expected to influence a limited number of subordinates by their actions. Deputy Store Manager and Store Manager were required to improve the whole "store" operation so they needed to train every single staff to practice "basic behavior" and CS practices. Therefore, relations with subordinates were also one of the significant factors for their promotion.

The operational evaluation check sheet had three major internal evaluators including the Store Manager, the Supervisor, and the Operations Manager from the Store Operations Department, and the external evaluator indicated the team members of the internal audit. The latter was external in the sense that they worked for the Greater China Area and most of them had no longer work experience in Hong Kong. Subsequently, I will examine how the nature of evaluation has shifted from the day-to-day evaluation to the "momentary/impression evaluation" (shunkan hyōka) along with the increase of their ranks.

Employees who were ranked lower than Deputy Store Manager needed to be selected and recommended by the Store Managers first. Store Managers were supposed to consult employees during the monthly face-to-face meeting about their future promotion opportunities and then help subordinates to make a practicable plan by analyzing the weakness of each promotional candidate. When the deadline for the plan came, employees met Store Managers and talked about their evaluations. Store Managers were supposed to observe subordinates every day, thus, making it easier for them to identify whether the promotional candidates achieved what they have promised. If the result satisfied the Store Manager, employees were able to obtain a formal recommendation from the Store Manager. They then needed approval from the Supervisor and then the Operations Manager.

The difference was observed between the employees who were ranked above the Senior Salespersons and those who were ranked lower. The Operations

Manager personally checks if the Senior Salesperson or above-ranked employees were qualified while lower-ranked employees normally passed this step directly to the written examination. Therefore, even though candidates gained recommendations from both Store Managers and Supervisors, they would not be qualified without the approval from the Operations Manager.

Employees who were ranked above S3 needed approval from the internal audit team members before the written examination in addition to the approval from the Supervisor and the Operations Manager. The internal audit was conducted by the top higher-ranked employees who worked for the Greater China Area. During fieldwork, I found that the team members were all Japanese. Most of them worked a relatively long time at Ichi and were experts in store operation including visual merchandising display, layout, and inventory control. They usually visited the store once a month and tended to visit the higher-ranked stores. They informed the Head Office before their visit; however, they occasionally visited without prior notice. The time of the visit of the internal audit team members varies. They might visit during the preparation before the opening or during the opening hours. Visits in general are accompanied by local directors of the office department and the Japanese Operations Manager.

Evaluation criteria of the internal audit followed the Operations Evaluation Check Sheet; however, local Store Managers observed three major promotional criteria for Store Managers (S2) and those who were ranked above: sales, the practice of CS, and subordinate training. There were twofold evaluations: impression and non-impression. Before visiting the store, internal audit members referred to the "number" and the result of these three criteria. The sales were the obvious criterion to evaluate if the Store Manager "well" managed the stores. In this sense, the higher-ranked stores with higher sales gained a strong advantage compared with lower-ranked stores. Evaluation of the practice of CS could be done by the results of the monthly CS checkup, which will be further explored later. Subordinate training could also be evaluated through the "number" of promoted subordinates. Another was on the impression evaluation meaning what the team members observed and felt on the day of the visit. Among these three criteria, the most obvious criterion was the practice of CS and subordinate training as internal audit team members were able to observe if their subordinates achieved a higher level of CS or if they followed kijun (standard) at the store.

Impression evaluation was designed to offer objective evaluation. The founder worried about how "human relations" within the company might result in unequal evaluation. Therefore, higher-ranked employees who played a significant role in the company's operation had to be evaluated equally without any subjective issues. This type of evaluation is a cost-saving remedy for the internal audit team members as they had to fly to other areas to give evaluation within a limited time.

The result of the internal audit was important in the sense that Store Managers who were ranked C-rank more than three times would be demoted for one rank, a practice that was not common among Japanese retailers. Moreover, the founder decentralized great authority to the team members, and their reports of the Store Managers worldwide were directly sent to the founder who had the final decision-making power. There was a case when a local Store Manager in Hong Kong was ranked a C-rank and Sakai decided to demote him based on the result offered by the internal audit team.

CS Check Sheet was the basic requirement for all employees so everyone had to meet requirements. The major principle of Ichi, or in many other Japanese retailers, focuses on the strong emphasis on the role of customer service as the more customers are satisfied with the service, the higher their chances of them to purchase more products, which could increase annual sales. Therefore, employees should significantly achieve a higher level of customer satisfaction. As part of the "Global One" policy, Ichi made a list of standard requirements of customer service, which was intended to achieve a higher level of CS. The company believed that if all employees in any region or country behaved according to this list, achieving a higher level of CS is possible.

The CS Check Sheet has nine parts, namely, greetings, prohibited behaviors, care for customers, responding to requests, cash registers, fitting rooms, alternation, cleaning, and telephone etiquette, with one to five requirements in each part. Each requirement accounted for 2 to 4 points. The evaluation was ranked in total at four levels from A, the best, to D, the worst based on their total points. The A-rank was above 85 points, B-rank ranged between 65 and 84 points, C-rank ranged between 45 and 64 points, and D-rank was lower than 44 points.

The major characteristic of this check sheet was its intention to use the practice of CS to link Ichi with the "Japanese-alike" culture. Politeness, smiling, or the so-called hospitality for customers was regarded as the major features of hospitality in Japan. Reisinger and Turner (1999:1221) described that politeness was the ideological aspect of Japanese culture and was an expression of decent manner as a way to avoid public conflict. Another was setting the part of "Prohibited Behaviors" to list up behaviors that might "damage" the image of the company. There were not only inappropriate behaviors toward the customers but also inappropriate words from employees. This behavior could be interpreted as the shame culture of Japan. According to Takie Lebra (1983: 194), the distinctive feature of Japanese culture was its sensitivity to superficial shame or embarrassment. To avoid behaviors related to the "shame" of the company, the store employees were required to practice good behavior.

These characteristics were superficial in the sense that the company expected customers to "see" the performance of employees' Japanese-alike CS. This intention required employees to "present" themselves to the customers rather than using their own interpretation of hospitality. Therefore, the company was reluctant to explore the localized way of CS or to expect employees to perform from the heart but rather to unify the image of the Ichi brand as a "Japanese-alike" one.

Another characteristic was the ambiguous definition of some concepts, whereby the result might be subjective; for example, the definition of "smile," "polite," and "inappropriate words" were quite ambiguous in the sense that every evaluator might interpret these concepts differently. Even though the company listed some examples of "inappropriate words," every situation is different.

Internal evaluation comprised four major evaluators, including the CS team members, the Store Manager, Supervisor, and the Operations Manager; whereas only one external evaluator, the mystery shoppers. External evaluation, which was used as mystery shoppers, did not belong to the local subsidiary but outsourced by the subsidiary in mainland China.

One of the distinctive features of a mystery shopper was that its impression evaluation reinforced the "presentation" of employees. Similar to the case of internal audit, this practice also intended to offer an objective assessment. However, the nature of the check sheet allowed employees to disguise their practice of CS. Therefore, candidates needed to "show" their practice of CS whenever necessary. Employees who were ranked lower than a Store Manager (S2) needed to present themselves to the Store Managers and the CS team members. However, given the limited time for the CS checkup and their nature of multifunction, the result might be distorted.

Another feature was that employees ranked above Store Managers (S2) needed collaboration from subordinates as their promotion was based on the overall performance of store employees. The evaluation of Store Managers (S2) and those who were ranked above required collaboration from subordinates to practice standardized CS as they were evaluated through the overall performance of store employees. This type of evaluation would benefit the subordinates who largely relied on the Store Managers for their promotion opportunities.

Written Examination

After obtaining the approval from superiors, the promotion candidates took a written examination, the content of which varied for each rank. Two types of questions were provided: multiple-choice and fill-in-the-blank questions. Multiple-choice questions covered a wide range of topics. The contents were based on the Operations Evaluation Check Sheet, the company's principles, and company manuals. Ichi believed that every task should have standard procedures and purposes. Therefore, employees were trained to memorize all procedures and purposes in the company manuals and practiced at stores. While Full-time and Advanced Salespersons were required to memorize the staff manual that included basic front-line work, the Senior Salespersons and above employees were tested on the contents of the Employee Manual which explained front-line work in detail and included managerial work. The Store Manager had to take an examination based on the Store Manager's manual which included fewer pages than the employee's manual and focused more on employee management and sales.

Fill-in-the-blank questions mainly required candidates to memorize every detail of the company principles. The company's principles were divided into two categories, the first one was the principle of the company; another included the principles of the stores. The principles of Ichi included its statement, its mission, its value, and so on. Employees were also required to write down all related principles at stores, such as "Ichi Basic Policy" and "Three Promises." These types of questions had a strict requirement and any wrong character or punctuation was counted as a mistake and received no points.

Interview

The final part of their promotional examination comprised a series of interviews. Any level of promotional interviews involved two employees: the director of the Human Resources Department and the Operations Manager from the Store Operations Department. The higher the ranks of employees were, the higher number of interviewers attending the oral examination; for example, employees who were ranked above Senior Salesperson candidates had to conduct interviews with the CEO of Hong Kong. The contents of the interview questions also differed. For the promotion interviews of Full-time Salesperson, the contents focused more on their career path in the future and self-development; whereas, for that of the Advanced Salespersons, the interviewers wanted to learn how candidates trained subordinates and achieved self-development. Candidates for higher-ranked employees above Senior Salespersons would have to answer questions related to the actual number, such as the total sales, to examine how well they knew the company's operation. Store Manager (S2) candidates might be asked to describe their contribution to the specific stores. For Store Manager (S3) candidates, interviewers wanted to learn the degree of their contribution to the area that the store belonged to and they interviewed in Shanghai with the senior higher-ranked employees of the Greater China Area. Supervisor candidates were expected to contribute to the whole company. By the end of 2012, no local Supervisors had attended an interview for the promotion in Hong Kong. However, interviewers usually passed the interviews as the candidates had the endorsement from recommenders. In other words, the status and reputation of the nominators played a significant role in the interviews of the candidates. Therefore, it was rare for candidates, especially for lower-ranked full-timers, to be rejected for promotion at the stage of the interview.

The above description of written examination and interview had several implications. First, the requirement of memorizing the company manuals and the company principles enhanced the importance of form as the major role of employees was to write from memory. It also allowed employees to know what is crucial for the promotion assessment and what is not necessary, which allowed the "presentation of self." Second, the status and reputation of the nominators played a significant role in the interviews of the candidates. Interview for promotion was close to a format rather than an actual examination as candidates already had endorsement from their superiors so they were supposed to be qualified for promotion.

Promotion in the informal practice is described in the next section attempting to illustrate the features that will be described above particularly focusing on how the subordinates practiced getting approval from their superiors on one hand and how the Store Manager encouraged subordinates to collaborate with them on the other.

Promotion in Practice

This section shows a picture of how the promotion of store employees is practiced at the East Point City (EPC) store and how the individual "presentation of self" has developed into the "collaborative performance" along with the increase of their rankings.

Three distinctive, influential key persons were in charge of selecting candidates during the actual promotional process: the Store Manager, Jenny, the local Supervisor of the EPC store, Mark, and the Japanese Operations Manager, Mizuno. Although these persons played a very important role in the employees' promotion, their respective roles were not the same. As the Store Manager worked with promotional candidates frequently and knew them very well from the work front, the Supervisor and the Operations Manager only know the promotional candidates through occasional store visits which are based on the informal store ranking and their priorities.

Jenny is one of the Store Managers at the EPC store. She worked at the store from March 2010 to January 2011, and she was assigned to open a new store in Olympian City. She was recruited to be one of the mid-career senior local Store Managers. Her reluctance toward her promotion and that of her subordinates is her major characteristic.

Mark, the Supervisor, is one of the most influential local employees at Ichi Hong Kong. He was the second most senior member of the local staff. He was promoted to Supervisor in 2008, and he is the only employee in Ichi who got promoted to that position within three years. He clearly knows the company's requirements because of his long years of service.

The Japanese Operations Manager, Mizuno used to work at two different companies in Japan before entering Ichi. After the first company went bankrupt, he worked in a hotel for one year. Mizuno claimed he loved serving customers and enjoyed training subordinates. In October 2000, Mizuno joined Ichi as a mid-career. Ichi was not as big and famous then as it is now, and the senior manager and subordinates had a closer relationship. He recalled that he was surprised the top manager came for the third round of face-to-face interviews. He was promoted to Store Manager within one year and to Store Manager (S3) two years later. After one more year, he was promoted to Supervisor. Mizuno was then relocated to Hong Kong in March 2008 and worked as an Operations Manager for his outstanding ability and leadership. His partner left Hong Kong two years later, and Mizuno had to take care of the general policy and store visits. Mizuno was too busy to conduct as frequent store visits as he wished.

Lower-Ranked Employees: Individual "Presentation of Self"

From Full-time Salesperson (F1) to Senior Salesperson (F3), the "presentation of self" of an individual is compulsory to obtain the recommendation of the Store Manager and the approval of the Supervisor. The so-called "presentation of self" is not giving a speech or presenting something at a certain place. The phrase refers to one's working behavior, particularly their behavior toward customers, which is judged by the Store Manager and Supervisor. The software-related skills, such as the practice of CS, are an important criterion in judging qualified candidates from lower-ranked employees, who were supposed to have the required hardware-related skills such as the Ichi standards of the shop floor.

I shall take two examples to understand the situation on site and see the different ways of "presentation of self" are practiced. These examples are Sabrina, a Full-time Salesperson, and Helen, an Advanced Salesperson. I will show how Sabrina got a promotion by "presentation" her improved CS performance to the Supervisor, Mark, after the first failure. I will also show why Helen, a staff who is good at "presentation", could be promoted with the support of the Japanese top manager.

Sabrina entered Ichi in 2007 as a Full-time Salesperson when the EPC store opened. Being punctual and hardworking, Sabrina was not so good at greeting people with a smile. She was not promoted for the first time since the Supervisor, Mark, did not recommend Sabrina because Mark believes that employees who cannot smile at colleagues cannot smile at customers; one who cannot accept this belief cannot be promoted. Sabrina received "advice" from the Store Manager regarding this issue and colleagues telling her that the promotional candidates in Ichi have to smile and greet not only customers but also their superiors. Sabrina tried to smile as much as possible and started to greet Mark whenever he comes to visit the store. Thanks to her "hard effort", Sabrina got a recommendation and was promoted in 2010.

Unlike Sabrina, the promotion of Helen was smoother. She joined Ichi in 2009 and was relocated to the Kowloon Bay store with support from the Japanese Operations Manager, Mizuno, one year later. She was promoted to Advanced Salesperson soon and was relocated to the store in Taipo several months later. Aside from Mizuno, Helen was also favored by other superiors. For instance, Taguchi who replaced Mizuno as the Operations Manager in 2012 gave high scores for Helen's "proper" work performance.

Helen said her "presentation" to Taguchi was in fact very dramatic and accidental. One day when Helen was still an Advanced Salesperson, the Store Manager took a day off and the Assistant Store Manager was left in charge of the night shift. The Assistant Store Manager was supposed to take control of the progress of every staff to finish the task on time. However, he spent too much time on his task in the back room. Thus, no manager was on the sales floor. When Helen noticed the situation, she decided to do some of the tasks of the Assistant Store Manager and finish her task at the same time. At the time she was managing subordinates and checking the store operation, Taguchi suddenly came to the store and found Helen concentrating on her work, serving customers very warmly, and keeping things in order with earnest. Taguchi was surprised to learn that Helen was just an Advanced Salesperson but helped with the task of the Assistant Store Manager. This good impression made Taguchi pay more attention to Helen, including her promotional opportunity, which resulted in her successful promotion from Advanced Salesperson to Senior Salesperson.

Both the "presentation of self" of Sabrina and Helen for promotion showed the need for CS and the importance of daily work attitude which could be observed and judged more objectively by the Store Manager but less by the Supervisor because of few visits. This situation can be a serious problem for some because the impression of the Supervisor could be too subjective sometimes. Imagine if Helen did not help the Assistant Store Manager the day when the Operations Manager came; she could have missed the chance to present herself to the higher-ranked employees, which could have delayed her promotion. What I would like to stress is that the judgment of the Supervisor about the "presentation" of employees could not always be correct and believable. If the "presentation of self" is considered necessary for lower-ranked employees, the judgment of the Store Manager should be more important because he works with employees on the site.

Transition Stage: Necessity of Collaboration from Colleagues

The transition stage includes the Senior Salesperson and Management Trainee who want to be an Assistant Store Manager. The case of Kelvin the Senior Salesperson can show that more attention was paid to the "collaborative" performance of evaluators regarding the issue of hardware skills such as Ichi standards, which directly influenced the sales of the store in contrast to the indirect influential practice, such as the practice of CS.

By contrast, the case of Gina the Management Trainee shows that the system of the company to encourage the training of Management Trainees allowed her to be promoted even if many employees, including the Store Manager, believe her job ability is quite low.

Kelvin was born in Hong Kong in 1986 and has an older sister, who lives near the EPC store. Kelvin started as a part-time salesperson at the Festival Walk store while he was still a student in a vocational school. When he was still working part-time, the Store Manager encouraged him to work full-time after his graduation, and Kelvin took his advice. He became a Full-time Salesperson after working part-time for one year. The Store Manager paid much attention to their promotion of Kelvin and gave him opportunities to learn as many new things as possible. Kelvin worked hard and was promoted to Advanced Salesperson after one year, and he was relocated to the EPC store. Employees at the EPC store gave high scores when evaluating the job ability and professional skills of Kelvin, who was even considered more competent than the Assistant Store Manager, Gina. For questions, employees ask Kelvin instead of the Assistant Store Manager. With their working attitude and rich experience, Kelvin gradually built up his status and reputation among employees at the store. Other employees consider Kelvin as a staff who has a higher emotional quotient (EQ).

A good relationship with colleagues and superiors is very important for promotion in Ichi. Kelvin knows it quite well, and he mentioned a couple of times during my interview that the standard of the shop floor largely depends on the motivation and cooperation of employees, including part-time employees. Thus, conflict with colleagues should be avoided and regular communication with them should be maintained. Kelvin regularly talks with colleagues on the shop floor and attempts to find out their current problems at work. Even the Store Manager and Assistant Store Manager who care less about human relations within the store asked Kelvin to act as a critical mediator between employees and managers. Kelvin won the understanding and collaboration of his colleagues, which in turn helped him pass the assessment for promotion.

Aside from keeping a good relationship with other employees, Kelvin also made conversations with superiors. Many EPC employees are afraid to even look at their superiors, but Kelvin talks and jokes with the Store Managers and Supervisors because he clearly understands the importance of their support for his promotion. He said, "My future career path depends on what the Store Manager tells Supervisor Mark about my performance. Mark is not coming to the store every day. So the information from the Store Manager means everything to him." Kelvin thinks Mark is a realistic man and is desperate to see the result. Therefore, showing concrete development that can give Mark a deep impression is important.

After working for six months at the EPC store, Kelvin was recommended to take the promotional examination for an Assistant Store Manager, which was approved by Mark, the Supervisor. Mizuno, the Operations Manager, came to the store to assess Kelvin's qualifications. Afterward, Mizuno announced that Kelvin was not qualified enough to be promoted because he failed to manage the inventory control and overtime work well. He missed the replenishment of the necessary item and placed the property. Moreover, he allowed employees to work relatively long overtime work. Insufficient replenishment influenced the sales and increased the workload of other employees. Regarding overtime work, it shows a low ability to achieve the expected job efficiency.

Kelvin worked and maintained a stable relationship with colleagues as usual in the following three months until he got promoted. Kelvin said he did not learn any new skills within those three months because he already learned those skills that got him a promotion before the first recommendation. He added that a more stable relationship with colleagues might have implicitly contributed to better result.

The case of Kelvin implies that his promotion needed cooperation from skillful and motivated colleagues, who played a significant role in his promotion because he cannot cover all the tiny details every day. To gain strong support from the subordinates, Kelvin used his rich experience and high social skills or, as store employees put it, high EQ to build his status and maintain a relatively stable and good relationship with colleagues.

The Assistant Store Manager, Gina entered Ichi in 2010 as Management Trainee and was first assigned to the EPC store. Gina is interested in painting and photography and loves art and enjoys going to museums; thus, she wanted to work in a related industry. After graduating from a private university in Hong Kong, she only got an offer from Ichi.

Unlike the Senior Salesperson, Kelvin, Management Trainee including Gina, is backed up by the Head Office because they are considered future Store Managers by Ichi, and the Store Managers were mainly responsible for their training. The promotion speed for Management Trainees has changed over time. For instance, a previous Management Trainee at the EPC store spent more than two years becoming an Assistant Store Manager. However, the goal when Gina was in training to get promoted within half a year. In 2010, all fresh Management Trainees were promoted to Assistant Store Manager after a three-month probation period. Although they were promoted to Assistant Store Manager, their functional job titles do not always consistent with their job abilities. Jenny, the Store Manager, was reluctant to give OJT to Gina and generally ignores her since OJT normally results in additional overtime work for the Store Manager. Jenny mainly assigned Gina to different locations to learn basic front-line work and gave her less opportunity to learn managerial skills which Gina needed for passing the probation period. One day, Keith, an Advanced Salesperson who worked at Ichi for more than two years, and Gina were assigned to be responsible for the night shift, the Store Manager did not hesitate to pass the unfinished tasks to Keith, who was ranked lower than Gina. Michelle, the former Deputy Store Manager at the EPC store commented that the attention of the Store Manager plays a more significant role in the training of Management Trainees.

However, Jenny recommended Gina for promotion to Assistant Store Manager as other Store Managers did after three months. Gina was promoted although she has a poor level of skills and insufficient cooperation from colleagues. This is ironic in the sense that Kelvin, a Senior Salesperson who has rich skills and maintains a stable relationship with colleagues was rejected to be promoted because of his "poor" skills and "less" collaboration from colleagues.

The case of Gina and Kelvin indicates that the power of the corporate system could not be overestimated. Ichi's strong intention on the company building issue results in the standardization of its corporate system which has promotional privileges for Management Trainees in Hong Kong. Therefore, the possible inequality for employees who do not have university diploma is less emphasized.

Store Managers: Collaborative Performance by Subordinates

The promotion of employees who were ranked higher than Store Manager (S2) reinforces the collaborative performance of subordinates. At this stage, the leadership and ability of candidates to keep the whole store together are more important. At the same time, the company should train subordinates who are persistent in following the company manual and can solve problems in any situation. For example, the case of Fiona, a Store Manager (S2) at the City Plaza store, shows how she motivates employees to improve the CS checkup by mystery shoppers and cooperation from "cooperative" subordinates, which are major criteria for the promotion.

Among Store Managers (S2) who were promoted to Store Manager (S3) by the end of 2012, Fiona has the fewest years of service and is the only Management Trainee. Fiona was born in 1985 and majored in Chinese at the Chinese University of Hong Kong. When she was studying, she hoped to be a Management Trainee at a global group involved in various fields including property development, marine, and air services. She was also interested in working at Cathy Pacific Airways, an aviation company of John Swire & Sons (H.K.) Ltd. Similar to other local students, the bank giant Hong Kong and Shanghai Banking Corporation Ltd. was also one of her options. However, Fiona received an offer only from Ichi, but she recalled it might be the right choice to make.

Most stores Fiona had worked at have ranked A. She was first assigned to the City Plaza store as a Management Trainee. Six months later, she was relocated to the Miramar store. After another six months, she was transferred to the Kowloon Bay store, which was closed two months later because the largest Ichi store was opened in the other building of the same shopping mall. Fiona helped open the new store as an Assistant Store Manager. After ten months, she was promoted to Store Manager, but she was reassigned to the City Plaza store where she was promoted to Deputy Store Manager. In October, the former Store Manager at the City Plaza store was transferred to Kwun Tong to help open a new store. Fiona was then promoted to Store Manager at the City Plaza store. After approximately six months, Fiona was transferred to the Miramar store again and worked with another local Store Manager (S3).

Fiona is well known by Ichi employees for her outstanding practice of CS, especially for her smile to customers and employees and her greetings on the sales floor. Although she claimed her promotion speed was slower than that of other Store Managers, the Head Office employees have high expectations from her because some top Japanese managers favored and considered her to be a Supervisor in the future. Fiona also wants to show the multilayered face of the store she manages because she dislikes other Store Managers, especially the senior ones, trying to "show" the practice of CS through the full preparation with mobilization of subordinates before the store visit of a superior. Although she is against such behavior, Fiona admits the importance of the positive result of a CS checkup contributed by collaborative performance. As a Store Manager, Fiona sometimes felt to be in a dilemma between following the manual of the company closely and her ideas. However, keeping the store at a high rank by any means, which was closely related to her promotion, is always clear to her. This idea was enhanced after the City Plaza store got an A-rank without a large staff reshuffle and additional training one month after it got a C-rank. Within that one month, Fiona tried her best to encourage subordinates before the CS checkup and used store meetings to enhance the team spirit after the unexpected low assessment.

Fiona was lucky that the level of CS and annual sales of the City Plaza store were high before she became the Store Manager. The Operations Manager even praised the level of CS of the store and gave a "very good" remark. Fiona knew that collaborative performance is needed to keep this good record, and she tried to achieve the higher goals. Unlike the previous Store Manager, Fiona encouraged their subordinates daily and showed that the result totally depends on the support of her subordinates. During the morning briefing session, Fiona always thanked the subordinates first. In one of these morning briefing sessions, she said:

> In the last week, we were able to achieve the target sales. This would never happen without everyone's supports. I know clearly that some employees only take 1-hour break even though they worked from 8 am to 8 pm, which really impressed me. I understand that all of you work very hard for a long time. If you ever felt tired or uncomfortable and need a replacement, please do not hesitate to ask me. I will replace you so that you could have a little break. I really do not want to see you guys tired. Let me be tired.

Fiona showed her understanding and gratitude for the devotion of employees to their work. She also maintained face-to-face meeting with subordinates to know their needs and thoughts regarding promotion and give them timely help and advice. This practice not only encouraged employees to work harder, but also to follow Fiona willingly in a practical job. The employees did not feel tired of memorizing the manual of company when Fiona asks them to. Higher-ranked employees at the City Plaza store carefully looked after the shop floor and quickly responded to the problem caused by disobedience to the manual of company. Ordinary employees were quite familiar with the formal requirements of the company and tried to put them into practice. Their devotion to work was caused by both their promotional interests and pride in working at the City Plaza store. I clearly remember when a part-time employee from the EPC store was assigned to temporarily work at the City Plaza store. The employee has long hair but she has never had it up at the EPC store; she took the habit with her to the City Plaza store. A Management Trainee saw her and said, "I know you do not need to hair up at the EPC store, but you have to do at *our* store." Everybody at the City Plaza store believes that their hard work is worthy of higher evaluation, and they had kept this record for a relatively long time. Therefore, they were shocked to learn they got a C-rank for the CS checkup in October 2011, which is the lowest rank for the City Plaza store. The score shocked Fiona and everyone, and they were anxious to know the reason.

C-Grade in October 2011

A mystery shopper visited the City Plaza store at about 8 pm during the Halloween Festival and gave a low score. This evaluation is the first monthly CS checkup after Fiona became the Store Manager. One could imagine how much Fiona was shocked.

Fiona organized a store meeting in mid-November to look for possible reasons for the C-rank in the CS checkup. They analyzed the result sheet and found that low ranking resulted from a lack of employees greeting customers at the entrance and also from unfriendly looking of the employees at cash registers and on the sales floor. Moreover, mystery shoppers pointed out that none of the staff at cash registers used one of the "Six Magic Words", "Sorry for keeping you waiting."

It turned out that Fiona was not working that night, and Martin, the Deputy Store Manager, was in charge. Fiona owned the responsibility, shared her feelings with pity, and encouraged subordinates by saying:

> Only Martin was present that day while I was playing *ghost* in Lan Kwai Fong (popular place for night life in Hong Kong) because of the Halloween Festival. As a Store Manager, I am responsible for this C-rank. When I got a phone call from Martin, I was surrounded by a number of *ghosts*. I could feel he was very upset. If you worked that day, you could have seen his facial expression. I certainly believe this result did not show our true daily standard, but we did what we should not do. I do hope the same thing will never happen in the future. I honestly have to say that some experienced employees performed worse even than new employees. I would like to know your opinion toward this result.

Everybody took the result very seriously. Some discussed the CS Check Sheet together while others studied the sheet carefully because they could not understand why they deserved such a result. Thomas, a Full-time Salesperson, asked Fiona about the comment made by the mystery shopper. Their conversation is as follows:

> THOMAS: The mystery shopper said that an employee did not close the door in the fitting room. What does that supposed to mean? I have never heard about this rule before.

FIONA: I have already argued or, in other words, quarreled about this with the superiors. Most mystery shoppers are from mainland China, and they do not quite know the differences between the operation there and in Hong Kong. Store employees are required to close the door for customers in mainland China, but no such requirement exists here. Maybe we have to show care about customers more by saying, "Please take care of your hands" or something like that.

IVY (ANOTHER FULL-TIME EMPLOYEE): We need to specify, such as "Please do not let your hands get caught in the fitting room door!"

(Everyone could not help laughing on Ivy's comment)

Most local employees felt performing what the company expects them to do in real work is difficult because the customers in Hong Kong care less about the *form* and seek service from the *heart*. For the company, a smile might not mean everything and the usage of language or pronunciation matters more. However, employees have to smile and greet every day the same as what the employees do in Japan to get a high evaluation of the "presentation of the store." To close the door of the fitting room for customers might look ridiculous to the locals. However, the mystery shopper from mainland China sees it as standard and qualified.

Like everyone in the store, Fiona was very upset with the C-rank because it greatly influences her future career. She is still a junior Store Manager and not satisfied, and she wishes for a promotion. As the key figure in the store, she was confident that she could get an A-rank in the future with all the employees and she expresses her confidence in her subordinates. She encourages employees and asked for the next goal of the store. A full-time employee said, "To get A-rank back!" and others showed their agreement by nodding, and their determination became solid. They began to look for where they should pay special attention, which Fiona identifies as performing well at the entrance because stores with the A-rank always pass this evaluation. After listening to Fiona's comment, some employees suggested how they could actually achieve this goal. Yuki, a full-time employee, said that even though no one stands at the entrance because of other tasks, they had to pay close attention to the entrance and greet loudly when anyone sees a customer coming. As long as an employee greets, all others have to repeat even if they did not see the customer. Everyone contributed ideas and helped build a strong team spirit despite the bad situation.

A-Grade in November 2011

The efforts of Fiona and other employees paid off. The City Plaza store got an A-rank in the CS checkup the following month. Although Fiona stressed she disliked the preparation for the checkup, she had to pay attention to the mystery shopper because she does not want the same bitter experience. Fiona told her subordinates that a mystery shopper might arrive at any time during the last week of November.

On the 29th of November, Fiona was on the sales floor when she found a customer who seems to be a mystery shopper. The man followed her and watched her secretly and carefully instead of looking for products. She assumed that the man is the mystery shopper and took actions immediately. She pretended to talk on the phone but was using the walkie-talkie to tell all employees that the mystery shopper had arrived. Fiona did not have to tell the employees what to do because she and other higher-ranked employees have called employees' attention to the CS with a walkie-talkie on a daily basis. When everyone heard her voice on the walkie-talkie, they smiled, greeted, responded to customers, and walked around to see if any customer needs help.

When the CS checkup came out, Fiona expressed her gratitude for the cooperation and hard work of every employee during the briefing session. She announced that many employees were praised in the Checkup Sheet. Full-time Salespersons Ada and Keira got high scores for the CS, and Fiona and the Management Trainee, Brian were praised as good employees. When Fiona found out that the mystery shopper would like to make her one of the best examples, she felt very happy to be praised but, at the same time, sorry for the tricky preparation.

The dramatic improvement of CS checkup informed Fiona why many stores could gain an A-rank even if their daily practice of CS is of a lower standard. Fiona believes that most highly ranked Store Managers assume their promotion requires a collaborative presentation of the practice of CS. Fiona gradually understood that the result of the CS checkup could be manipulative because the result largely depends on the impression evaluation by mystery shoppers, who might interpret the criteria differently. Thus, their assessment could be distorted. To better show their practices of CS, Store Managers needed the support of subordinates who knew how to do the "presentation" together.

Fiona gained cooperation from her subordinates based on her own strategy. She made sure that the employees are encouraged daily, their pride for working at an A-rank store is stimulated, and gaining a high score in the CS checkup is properly counter-measured to emphasize this ideology. Every day, Fiona tried to take care of every member of the staff by giving warm words and showing she cares for their health and promotion. She is unpretentious toward her subordinates. Aside from being close to subordinates, Fiona avoided showing her educational status (university graduate) because most employees are non-university graduates and felt unequal toward the privilege of being a Management Trainee.

Fiona stimulated the prestige feeling of store employees at the City Plaza store when the C-rank was given. Many employees at the store were proud of working at a higher-ranked store and regarded themselves as those who practiced a higher level of CS in Ichi. Therefore, the C-rank seriously influenced their pride. Fiona agreed on this issue but publicly disagreed with the result to motivate employees to gain an A grade. Although lower grades might have hurt her pride, the C-rank largely influenced her career in Ichi. Turning the situation around can be a great advantage for her future promotion.

Of course, the preparation played a significant role in achieving a higher rank. The analysis was done by Fiona on how the store employees could gain better rank allowed store employees to focus on the specific practice rather than attempting to meet all requirements of the CS Check Sheet. Because of such preparation, the store employees felt more confident in their practice and they were well prepared to welcome the mystery shopper whenever he or she visits the store.

Conclusion

In this chapter, I described the nature of the formal system and how it formed informal practices. The nature of the promotion system has three distinctive features. First, the superior and subordinate mutually depend on each other. Thus, one's promotion relies largely on the work performance of the other. Higher-ranked employees needed cooperation from a wider range of employees. Lower-ranked employees depend on Store Managers for a recommendation, whereas Store Managers rely largely on the work performance of their subordinates to get a better evaluation. Second, the company expected employees to practice the *form* of standard manuals because the ultimate goal of Ichi is to build up a company based on the standard corporate system including the company manuals that were rationally designed; however, many criteria in the manuals were ambiguously defined. Third, higher-ranked employees were evaluated based on the impression of superiors, which prompted candidates to "present" in front of the superiors, and the ambiguity of promotion criteria reinforced this tendency. Moreover, the nature of the mutual dependency of employees requires higher-ranked employees to gain cooperative "presentations" from their colleagues.

Through the analysis of promotion in practice, I tried to show how employees behave when they shared similar goals and interpretations of the corporate system. I found that the involvement of store employees in the 'presentation' shifted from the individual level to the collective and collaborative level. Employees needed cooperation from colleagues to meet the requirement and increase their ranks, although they are not expected to master every aspect of Ichi skills. Store Managers who were considered the "ultimate" multifunctional experts are expected to train subordinates in all skills. I used the example of the dramatic change in CS checkup at the City Plaza store to show how a Store Manager gained collaborative motivation by uniting subordinates toward the same goal, gaining a higher grade in the CS checkup, by encouraging them on a daily basis, stimulating their pride, and offering a detailed strategy to achieve the goal. These strategies were workable because subordinates and a Store Manager implicitly share a similar interpretation of the corporate system: the result of the checkup influences promotions.

Similarly, we observed harmonized collaborative performance because of the ability of higher-ranked employees to seek cooperation from colleagues and subordinates; however, I admit that conflicts among employees exist because of their different interests. In the next chapter, I examine how Store Managers largely influence the interests and institutional culture of employees by creating their regimes based on different career orientations and variant means of managerial control.

References

Lebra, S.T. (1983) Shame and Guilt: A Psychocultural View of the Japanese Self. *Ethos*, 11(3), pp. 192–209.

Reisinger, Y., & Turner, L. (1999). A Cultural Analysis of Japanese Tourists: Challenges for Tourism Marketers. *European Journal of Marketing*, 33(11/12), pp. 1203–1227.

8 Store Managers and Their Kingdoms

In the previous chapter, I pointed out how corporate ideology influences the behavior of employees and how candidates gained the collaborative presentation of subordinates for promotion. In the process of the company building of Ichi, Store Managers play a very important role. In this chapter, I focus on the role of Ichi Store Managers and how their different interpretation of corporate ideology, career orientations, and personal traits, create their own regimes, and transform human relations. There were many studies discussing how employees made sense of the messages delivered by the top management (Kezar, 2013; Maitlis, 2005; Weick, 1995), however, studies on the role of ideology have been underdeveloped (Mills et al., 2010). Corporate ideology, from their perspectives, includes two contents: sales and the practice of customer service (CS), and their interpretation and focus on these two contents differ. They have two career orientations, namely, aggressive or reluctant. In each regime, I analyze what drives them to pursue a particular corporate ideology and I also show the picture of the dynamic of complex human relations in five stores.

To better understand each regime, I will provide general background information about Store Managers before moving to a detailed description of their regimes. Jenny and Lisa were two local female Store Managers, whereas Utada, Nakamura, and Kaneko were three male Japanese Store Managers in August 2012 (see Table 8.1). The three male Japanese Store Managers were sent to Hong Kong as part of the practices of "Global One" to train junior Store Managers and improve store operations. Their evaluations were conducted biannually, and they are sent back to Japan if they failed to meet the requirement.

The rank of the Japanese Store Managers is S3, whereas the local Store Managers are ranked S2. Most Japanese Store Managers were promoted to S3 after three to four years of service. They were in their 30s and have been working for more than eight years in Ichi. The local Store Managers have been working for five years. All Store Managers are married, and three of them have children. Lisa, the local Store Manager, is the youngest parent among all Store Managers.

DOI: 10.4324/9781003305675-8

Table 8.1 Personal traits of five Store Managers, August 2012

Rank	*Name*	*Birth*	*Sex*	*Nationality*	*Education*	*Year of entry*	*Entry rank*	*Career development in Hong Kong*
S3	Kaneko	1976	M	Japan	University	2000	Management trainee	1. Mar 2011 - Aug 2011: New Town Plaza (with Yu) 2. Sep 2011 - Feb 2012: New Town Plaza (with Lisa) 3. Mar 2012 -Telford
S3	Utada	1978	M	Japan	High school	2001	Full-time salesperson	1. Mar 2011- Apr 2011: EPC (with Lisa) 2. Apr 2011- Jun 2011: Tuen Mun (with James) 3. Jul 2011- Aug 2011: EPC (with Lisa) Sep 2011- Sent back to Japan
S3	Nakamura	1981	M	Japan	University	2004	Management trainee	1. Mar 2011- Aug 2011: Plaza Hollywood (with Tusi) 2. Sep 2011- Feb 2012: City Plaza (with Fiona) & EPC (with Yu) 3. Mar 2012 - Tuen Mun
S2	Jenny	1977	F	Hong Kong	High school	2007	Senior salesperson	1. Sep 2007 - Feb 2010: Lee Theatre 2. Mar 2010 - Feb 2011: EPC 3. Mar 2011 - Aug 2012: Olympian City
S2	Lisa	1982	F	Hong Kong	High school	2007	Full-time salesperson	1. Sep 2007 - Aug 2008: Telford Plaza 2. Sep 2008 - Feb 2009: Plaza Hollywood 3. Mar 2009 - Aug 2010: World Trade Center 4. Sep 2010 - Feb 2011: New Town Plaza 5. Mar 2011 - Aug 2011: EPC (with Utada) 6. Sep 2011 - : New Town Plaza (with Nakamura)

Created by the author.

In terms of educational background, three of the five Store Managers have no university diploma, which has influenced their entry rank. Kaneko and Nakamura were promoted to Store Manager (S2) within one year because their university diploma allowed them to start their career with a higher rank. By contrast, Utada started as a Full-time Salesperson and was promoted to Store Manager (S2) within three years. In general, they were promoted to Store Manager (S3) after three to four years. Jenny entered the company as Senior Salesperson, and she was promoted to Store Manager (S2) three years later. Lisa started at the lowest sales position, and she was promoted to Store Manager (S2) after four years.

The career development of these Store Managers in Hong Kong is different. Kaneko and Nakamura passed the first biannual assessment and worked as trainers in one and three stores, respectively. They then worked in another store as a single Store Manager. Utada was relocated into two different stores with two local Store Managers within six months, which is a rare case. Local Store Managers are supposed to train employees, including fresh and junior Store Managers. The distinctive feature of trainees is that most local Store Managers are female and only Utada trained a male Store Manager. In this chapter, I will only focus on the period from March to December 2011.

The career path of the two local Store Managers differed in terms of the number of assigned stores. Jenny worked at the Lee Theatre for three years before she was relocated to the EPC store, whereas Lisa has been relocated to four different stores before working with Utada at the EPC store. Lisa has more experience working with different Store Managers and employees than Jenny.

The above background information showed different biographies of Store Managers and career development in Ichi. In the following sections, I analyze each Store Manager's regime starting with how their interpretation of the corporate ideology influenced their career orientation and management. The orientations can be divided into two categories, namely, aggressive and reluctant. Aggressive employees have a strong desire for promotion, whereas reluctant workers prefer to stay in the same position. I put Jenny under reluctant orientation and the four under aggressive orientation. In each regime, I show the dynamics of complicated human relations.

Jenny Regime: Reluctant Employees

Distinctive features of Jenny's regime are the transformation of power structure among subordinates because of Jenny's focus on the issue of CS, and "harmonious" human relations with the implicit conflict between Jenny and their subordinates.

Jenny was born in 1977. Among all Store Managers in Hong Kong, she has relatively longer years of service in Ichi by the end of 2011. She was married and her husband worked at a local company. She said she can have a child in the future and might consider resigning. Before coming to Ichi, Jenny worked as a salesperson at a local fashion retailer, Bossini, and moved as a Senior Salesperson at another local fashion giant, Giordano. She resigned at Giordano because the company requires her to work early in the morning at the store, which is quite far from her apartment.

Jenny entered Ichi as a mid-career in 2007. She started as a Senior Salesperson at the Lee Theater store in Causeway Bay for three years. With a strong recommendation from the local Supervisor, she became the Store Manager and was assigned to work at the East Point City (EPC) store from the end of February 2010. Jenny was reluctant to become the Store Manager because she believes the workload is quite heavy and she wanted to avoid long working hours. Although Jenny has concerns, she eventually took the examination because she understood that employees in Ichi are not expected to stay in the same position forever; the employees are expected to develop their careers. She thinks her action might benefit her career in the future as she favored the local Supervisor.

Jenny worked at the EPC store from March 2010 to February 2011 after being promoted to Store Manager (S2). She has a strong desire to stay in the same rank rather than pursue a higher rank and her interpretation of CS and career orientation influenced her relationship with subordinates.

Transformation of the Power Structure

Jenny focused largely on the practice of CS because she clearly understood that one of the criteria for Store Managers to stay or to be promoted is the practice of CS. Thus, she attempted to use and focus on this to, at least, secure her current position. However, she neglected the sales issue because she was reluctant toward promotion. Improving the practice of CS at the EPC store was not an easy task. Most employees do not usually practice CS, and their consciousness toward this practice is poor; thus, changing their mindset within a short time is hard.

To achieve the goal, Jenny kept better relations with subordinates who practiced CS well but dislikes those who did not. For instance, two Full-time Salespersons, Chorus and Roy, were favored by Jenny during the daily operation. Jenny treated them with a kind attitude and frequently hangs out with them. She also praised them in front of others and she assigned them to manage a CS team, which was only assigned to employees who are ranked above the Advanced Salespersons.

By contrast, she publicly criticized employees who did not practice CS, particularly a Full-time Salesperson, Oliver who is rebellious toward Jenny. Jenny required Oliver to follow the "Ichi Style", but Oliver did not follow the order because of the strong pressure from Jenny. Moreover, Jenny has frequently asked him to smile at customers when he is working on the shop floor. When Jenny realized it is hard to ask Oliver to follow the requirement of Ichi is quite hard, she only assigned him to work in rooms without customers, such as the back room or alternation room. Susan, a part-time employee, had a similar experience. She is an experienced staff with rich skills at the store; however, customers have complained about her inappropriate attitude twice. She is also reluctant to smile. To avoid more complaints that can damage Jenny's reputation, she did not assign Susan to the locations with a higher rate of customer complaints, such as the cash register and fitting room, unless the store is short of human resources.

To reduce her workload, Jenny efficiently used her subordinates, particularly Michelle, the Deputy Store Manager, and Kelvin, the Senior Salesperson, for the issues of sales including layout, inventory control, and replenishment assignment. Jenny barely passed the higher-ranked managerial task to Gina, the Assistant Store Manager, who was promoted three months after her entry because of poor job ability. Before the Deputy Store Manager, Michelle was relocated in early 2011, Michelle and Kelvin deployed the workload of the Store Manager. After Michelle left, the authority largely transferred to Kelvin because of their poor job ability of Gina. Moreover, Jenny relied on Kelvin more. These changes increased the status of Kelvin as he replaced the Store Manager. Although their authority of Kelvin is great, he could not go beyond the boundary of the power of the Store Manager.

"Harmonious" Relations

In this section, I attempt to demonstrate how subordinates interact with Jenny "harmoniously" even though they implicitly disrespected Jenny for her reluctant work attitude and abuse of power.

Jenny did not hesitate to show her reluctance toward work or her disobedience to some company regulations regarding her subordinates. For instance, she goes to the comfort room many times during work hours; many employees see her frequently go to the toilet before the break, which prompted them to think that Jenny is trying to avoid work as much as possible. She also disobeyed some company regulations. For instance, employees are not allowed to eat during work hours, but Jenny eats something in the staff room. Once during my break, I buy fruit mix chips in the supermarket upstairs and bring them to the staff room. When I ate them, I asked Jenny if she wanted some because I delivered them to other employees who had break together. I did not expect Jenny would take them; however, she said they looked so interesting and ate them even though she was working. In the morning during the opening hours, I worked in the fitting room and went to the staff room for water. I heard Jenny ask Janet, an Advanced Salesperson who was going on a break soon, to buy "fish balls," a popular Hong Kong snack, for her. I was surprised to hear that since Jenny's break is not until two hours, which means she plans to eat something during work hours.

Despite her disobedience, Jenny strictly requires employees to follow company regulations. For instance, store employees are not allowed to put their water bottles on the refrigerator. One day, Jenny saw a filled McDonald's coffee cup up there and used her walkie-talkie to ask whose coffee cup that was.

After a female Full-time Salesperson confessed, Jenny warned all employees with the walkie-talkie. However, I found out later that she puts her own on top of the refrigerator.

When EPC store employees notice Jenny's attitudes and behaviors, they discuss them behind her back; however, none of them has ever tried to talk to the Supervisor or report the situation to the Head Office because she has the final decision and power over the issues of promotion and relocation. Moreover, Jenny might not be dedicated to her work, but she requires her subordinates to at least "show" that they followed Ichi requirements rather than to truly acquire or achieve the standard level of skills.

Jenny used her centralized authority to make decision and adjustment, such as in a change of schedule, as she wanted. For instance, during the opening preparation, she ordered the higher-ranked employees to do different managerial work but she stayed in the higher-ranked employees' room to revise the daily work schedule to move her break to a favorable time. To change the daily work schedule, she needed someone to take care of her work without gaining consent from the person. If she is unable to find a replacement, she would move more than one staff to meet her expectation. This conduct influences other employees. Nonetheless, Jenny does it frequently, and every employee knows what she does before the opening.

Many full-time and part-time employees understand this. Therefore, they did not expect Jenny could help them prepare before the opening. Most of them have barely thought to fight for their rights or ask the Store Manager to help them. However, they prefer to finish the work by themselves because of Jenny's ignorance of the issues on the sales floor; most employees prefer to solve problems themselves.

In addition, Jenny has power over the training of subordinates. She appreciated the job ability of most employees who are higher than Advanced Salesperson except Gina, the Management Trainee. In 2010, the company implemented the "Global One" policy. One of the requirements is to emphasize the training of Management Trainees; management training should not be neglected. However, Gina was offered less OJT because of Jenny's reluctance. Jenny did not only show her reluctance to her subordinates but also shared her feelings with other Store Managers. Once I took a taxi with Jenny and two other Store Managers in November 2010, and I heard Jenny complain about poor job ability of Gina. Jenny kept complaining although the other Store Managers did not comment.

Gina said that she is far from other Management Trainees, who have learned more skills than her. Nonetheless, the skill development of Gina was negatively influenced by Jenny, but she understood Jenny's intention. Gina chose not to be rebellious because Gina believes that she did not have to deal with Jenny soon as Management Trainees would be automatically relocated once a year.

Both full-time and part-time employees tend to obey the Store Manager because they want to avoid being scolded by Jenny, who treats them with a coercive attitude. However, the attitude of Jenny is different when talking to part-time employees who are skillful and new part-time employees who have limited skills. Some employees said Jenny's different attitude is because she does not value the latter. Moreover, Jenny sometimes scolded new part-time employees in front of others to show her authority and strictness. For instance, when I chat with other employees in the staff room during the break, Jenny scolded Tiffany, a new part-time employee, because she has too many requests for her working shifts. Jenny said loudly, "I ask you to give more working shifts, you cannot. I ask you to work overtime, you find other excuses. What is wrong with you?" Every staff at the room stopped chatting because of the intense ambiance. It was not her first time scolding Tiffany and we saw the Store Manager scold a new part-time employee. Nonetheless, Tiffany just apologized for her behavior and obeyed Jenny; however, she sometimes talked to other part-time employees about Jenny being unreasonable and her attitude toward part-time employees.

Many employees have an implicit conflict with Jenny, but most of them cannot speak out or be rebellious against Jenny. Instead, they only keep their distance from her. For instance, they do not prefer to take a break with Jenny. During my break with other Full-time Salespersons, one of them said Jenny went out for a lunch with the Supervisor so we could eat lunch in the staff room. Another day, an Advanced Salesperson found out she had to take a break with Jenny alone; she said she would like to die. However, full-time employees cannot refuse to go out and eat lunch with Jenny because of her strong authority within the store.

Some experienced part-time employees reacted reluctantly toward the Store Manager. One day, some part-time employees, including Keneeth who has been working for more than one year, talked in the staff room during the break. While Keneeth was loudly chatting with others, Jenny came in and told him his voice was too loud that customers outside could hear him. Keneeth only told the higher-ranked employees, "Oh, bye." Keneeth's response is surprising because only a few part-time employees behave like him. Keneeth said it does not matter because the Store Manager does not take it seriously. Moreover, Ken, another experienced part-time employee, walked slowly after he started working. Jenny saw him and asked him to move faster. However, Ken pretended he did not hear Jenny and continued walking slowly. Ken said that apart from the absence of a strict layoff policy of the company, he knows Jenny actually needs them because of labor shortage, where training new part-time employees are not cost-efficient.

Jenny's strong expectation of stability results in her lower motivation toward the training of subordinates. She particularly focuses on the practice of CS without paying attention to the increases in sales. Thus, higher-ranked managers, especially Senior Salesperson Kelvin, gained a high degree of autonomy. Subordinates endure reluctance and abuse of authority of Jenny, but they implicitly complain. Compared with the next regime, Jenny's regime is "harmonious" because of the lack of public conflict among subordinates, although most of them are less motivated.

Lisa Regime: Unique *Shōten* (Store)[1]

In Lisa's regime, I intend to show the picture of how the same groups of employees at the EPC store could behave differently from Jenny's regime because of the different management styles of Lisa who emphasized the sales issue and subordinate promotion.

Lisa was born in 1982. She is the youngest Store Manager without a university degree. She was married and had two children. She was described as a "strong mother" all the time by other employees. Before entering Ichi, Lisa used to run a fashion shop with her twin sister. She said they spent more time hanging out with friends than with family members. After giving birth to her second child, Lisa wanted more time with her family members and a more stable life, thus, she chose to work at Ichi. After working at the Telford store for one year, she was relocated to the Plaza Hollywood store, the World Trade Center store, and the New Town Plaza store. The last two stores are ranked A.

Both Jenny and Lisa were junior Store Managers and the EPC store was their first store. When Lisa arrived at the EPC store in March 2011, many employees noticed her difference from Jenny within several days. Although Lisa worked at the EPC store for only half a year, she had a strong influence on the transformation of the power structure among subordinates based on her focus on sales and subordinate promotion.

Focus on Sales and Subordinate Promotion

Lisa mainly focused on the sales floor, such as layout and store standards because she believes the sales floor is more important than CS. She formed a CS team and assigned several full-time employees to take care of the CS practices of employees, but she personally managed the issue less than Jenny. Moreover, Lisa did not push employees to practice CS unless it is necessary for their promotion. Therefore, the conflict between Lisa and part-time employees is less obvious than that of Jenny. Lisa would not usually talk to store employees except outside the workplace, but she sometimes consults them with regard to the issue of human relations within the store.

As Lisa described, she believed that sales are more important than CS for the store operation. Moreover, she did not require employees to practice CS because even she practiced it a little. Lisa required subordinates to pursue the attractive shop layout by making frequent adjustments. One day, Lisa came toward me and looked at the layout. She asked me to switch color because she thinks that the layout is unattractive. Moreover, she emphasized the importance of efficiency. She required employees to organize the equipment in the back room to increase job efficiency. She said pops and stickers, as well as equipment, were not organized. Moreover, she understood that the requirement of the previous Store Manager is unclear. She also carefully checked the sales floor before the opening, including pops and cleaning.

Lisa allowed more full-time employees to be promoted than Jenny did. She wanted to help as many employees as possible, and she asked the Supervisor whether a store is available so part-time employees can be relocated and become Full-time Salespersons. When Lisa conducts a face-to-face interview with store employees every month, she carefully learns what her subordinates wanted and tried her best to help them. When I wanted to be relocated, she helped me ask the Supervisor regarding any store available for me.

With her hard work, Lisa was considered to be a role model by store employees. For instance, when a full-time employee saw Lisa replenish the stock on the sales floor, she regarded Lisa as a role model for Store Managers. Unlike Jenny, Lisa was less fond of breaking the rule of the company. I never saw her eat anything during her work. She interacted more with front-line employees and allowed them to see how she worked in the store. Lisa sometimes sacrificed her break for work. For instance, she starts work five minutes earlier whenever she has lunch in the staff room.

Power Struggle Among Motivated Employees

Lisa focused on the issues on the shop floor and showed aggressiveness regarding the promotion of her subordinates, which prompted the reduced authority of the Senior Salesperson, Kelvin. Lisa prefers to make every judgment based on her idea. When Jenny was at the EPC store, the issues regarding layout were mainly handled by Kelvin. By contrast, Lisa prefers to do it on her own. Kelvin sometimes needs to revise the proposed layout according to Lisa. Moreover, Lisa started to assign tasks to other employees, which resulted in a reduced amount of tasks for Kelvin. Lisa believes promotion is the major concern of most less-motivated employees, so she gave many full-time employees opportunities to learn new skills to achieve qualification for promotion. Therefore, many candidates are not only eager to develop their skills but also show their development to Lisa to secure a promotion.

The power structure in Lisa's regime was represented by a power struggle between Gina, the Assistant Store Manager, and full-time employees. For example, the relationship between Gina and Kelvin gradually detached. Gina said Kelvin used to speak to her once or twice when they worked together. When Lisa was the Store Manager, he barely talked to her and ignored her. An experienced part-time employee said Kelvin and other higher-ranked employees dislike Gina, although he barely showed his feeling. When others say bad things about Gina, Kelvin usually keeps quiet and avoids commenting. Although Kelvin did not express his feelings toward Gina most of the time, he sometimes accused Gina of lacking her job ability. When I worked at the E block, I saw a customer who claimed the product has a problem and wanted to return it at the cash register. One of the cashiers reported this issue by walkie-talkie. However, no manager came to the cash register. Kelvin rushed to the cash register and helped the customer politely. When I went to the staff room to drink water, I heard Kelvin complain about Gina not answering the walkie-talkie. When the cashier called higher-ranked employees by walkie-talkie, Gina was working in the staff room as usual and claimed she heard nothing. Kelvin complained he was assisting a customer and was furious that Gina did not respond to the walkie-talkie. Gina was surprised by Kelvin's emotional behavior and told me later, "You see, Kelvin is so desperate to be promoted so he was not happy with anyone, and he never expresses his true feelings to us."

Besides the power struggle with Kelvin, Gina had a public conflict with Roy a Full-time Salesperson who was not able to adapt to the sudden changes regarding Gina being the learner to the person who only makes orders. With the bossy attitude of Gina, the two would sometimes have a conflict. Gina and Roy almost got into a big fight on the sales floor, where many customers were shopping. This major event is due to the dirty word "incident." In late December 2010, Roy said he had to have a meeting with Gina and the Store Manager one day. On the day of the meeting, Gina saw Roy, who did not greet her. Gina tapped him on the shoulder and said, "Hey, are you sick today?" Roy was furious to hear what she said and answered, "FXXX you." Gina was shocked to hear the word and ran to Lisa to relay the incident. Lisa looked for Roy and said they needed to talk. However, a talk did not happen that day. Several days later, Gina and Roy saw each other in the back room after their usual work. Gina confronted Roy to discuss and fix this issue, but Roy said he does not want to talk to Gina. Roy told me that day he those dirty words because he just wanted Gina to shut up.

After several weeks, Roy told me he would like to give up fighting with Gina and apologized. This incident did not only influence the relationship between Gina and Roy but also that between Gina and Janet, an Advanced Salesperson at the EPC store who dates Roy at that time. Janet blamed Gina for giving Roy overtime work so she cannot go to the theater with Roy that night. Janet heard Gina cry in front of the Store Manager and Roy, and said Gina deserves it.

Throughout Lisa's regime, the power structure among high-ranked employees changed because she focused on sales rather than the practice of CS. In addition, employees are highly motivated because Lisa talks about promotional opportunities, although Lisa keeps a "dry" relationship with subordinates. The subordinates of Lisa are ambitious; most of them want to show their development to Lisa to secure a promotion. Thus, they are usually in conflict with each other. Lisa's "dry" attitude toward her subordinates also reinforces the tendency for conflicts. In the next regime, I will describe the three cases of Japanese Store Managers, who have a similar career orientation but different managerial approach.

Utada Regime: Mission Incomplete

A major characteristic of Utada's regime is the gap between his effort to improve the practice of CS and incurred reluctance of local subordinates. I will first show the personal trait of Utada to offer his background information and then move to the explanation of why Utada focused more on the issue of CS. I will also discuss what strategy Utada used to motivate employees and what factors determined employees' reluctant attitudes.

Utada was in his late thirties. He came from the Saitama Prefecture, which is close to Tokyo. He had an older brother who works for a company. Utada was away from his parents when he was around 18 years old and seldom contacts his family members. He gave them his mobile phone number, but no one contacted him in the last three years. He did not go to a university and is called *pūtarō* (a person who did not have any job although he or she was supposed to). After being a "*pūtarō*" for some time, he worked as a *freeter* (a person without a full-time job except for housewives and students) in a convenience store and supermarket. He entered Ichi Japan as a Full-time Salesperson in 2000. Three years later, he became a Store Manager. Unlike most Japanese Store Managers in Hong Kong, Utada has never been transferred far from Tokyo. He lived with his wife in Tsim Sha Tsui, where the Japanese Operations Manager, Mizuno, also lives.

Utada worked at the EPC store from March 2011 to April 2011 and was relocated to the Tuen Mun store for two more months. He was relocated back to the EPC store for one month before he was sent back to Japan. I will mainly examine his relations with local employees at the EPC store.

Utada as "Enthusiastic Teacher"

Utada's enthusiasm for improving the practice of CS at the EPC store was strong because of two major reasons. The first reason is that the CS issue has always been a serious problem at the EPC store and the Japanese Operations Manager expected Utada could improve this situation. The lower ranking of the EPC store and the busyness of the Supervisor resulted in limited visits, which in turn resulted in employees' low motivation toward the practice of CS since employees have no one to "show" too. Another reason is that Utada did not have to spend too much time on the sales issue since the local Store Manager at the EPC store, Lisa had already taken good care of the issue even though Lisa was a junior Store Manager.

During the first month at the EPC store, he observed the practice of local employees and pointed out several major problems. Among various contents of CS, Utada especially focused on the "Ichi Style", smile, and the standard procedure. Utada used several methods with the hope that local employees could gradually change their consciousness toward CS. Utada discussed the issue with higher-ranked employees expecting them could transmit this idea to other employees. He also used the store meeting to express the importance of CS. Utada interacted with lower-ranked employees by complimenting them and attempting to improve their motivation.

Utada spent most of his time with the local Store Manager since he understood that only Lisa had the power to control employees. Utada respected

Lisa's territory and her management style, and at the same time, continued to persuade Lisa to focus on the practice of CS. Although their conflict was not apparent, we could observe their disagreement from their interactions.

One day, I had the opportunity to follow the work of Utada for three hours. After Utada completed checking the hardware of the shop floor, he asked the Store Manager to join the CS checkup with a check sheet. Utada tried to tell Lisa it was necessary to communicate with all staff about the importance of smiling and using compliments to improve their motivation. Although he was trying his best to persuade Lisa, it seemed she paid less attention to what he was saying. When they checked the practice of CS by employees, she only nodded to show her agreement toward Utada without giving any comments. While they were checking, Lisa received a phone call and did not show up for more than one hour.

The reason for Lisa's limited attention was mainly because she wanted to first take care of the hardware aspects of the store operation such as Ichi standard and then move to the software issues such as CS. However, from Utada's point of view, the shop floor was already quite stable, and thus, could not understand why Lisa could not move to the improvement of CS.

Most local subordinates agreed with Lisa's reluctant attitude toward the issue of CS even though Utada tried numerous ways attempting to change this situation. Take the recording for an instance. One day, during my break time, Utada showed a video that recorded employees' daily work to Gina, the Assistant Store Manager, Kelvin, the Senior Salesperson, and Lisa. While Utada was still explaining his findings from the video, Lisa walked away after a while as she was needed by employees on the shop floor. Although Utada was dissatisfied with Lisa's disinterest, he went on,

> I walked around shop floor as a customer, I looked around the products first, then I went to fitting room and finally I arrived at the cash register. Let me explain it by each stage. Although Mona was working at the A block where near the entrance, I could not see her from the entrance and neither did the customers. Ichi requires employees to be able to greet customers as they entered the store. Next was C block, which Lois is responsible for. I could not find her easily and more importantly, she did not practice CS. Moreover, you can see a number of D-rank situations. When I walked to the fitting room, I was surprised to see what was going on there. Janet, a Senior Salesperson, was busy responding to requests from customers and did not even see me. I saw two blue boxes full of products one on top of the other in front of the fitting room where customers could easily see. Moreover, because space is limited, it got the customers' way. But, I mean, it is not possible to see such picture in Japan even when we are busy. Japanese usually tend to hide "bad" things. I also found that employees did not treat products nicely. The last place I stopped by was the cash register. As usual, I observed that it lack sufficient number of workers. I suggested that Lois move to the fitting

> room and Janet should be at the cash register, because as you know, Ichi strongly emphasizes the role of cash register, which is the last stop for customers.

After Utada's analysis, Gina and Kelvin looked at each other and stated quietly that they were not surprised with what he observed as they were aware that employees did not practice CS although they were aware that they had to and knew the written contents of the CS Check Sheet. Kelvin and Gina did not share their opinion with Utada, instead, they stated that they would encourage to the other employees to practice more CS. At that time, Utada was confused about whether store employees knew the written requirements of the CS Check Sheet. He was not able to understand why local employees did not practice them even though they knew the requirement.

This reluctant attitude was not limited to the higher-ranked employees but also other full-timers. Take Utada's speech at the store meeting for instance. The last part of the meeting was hosted by Utada and I was asked to be his interpreter. Utada pointed out that a crucial part of achieving a higher level of CS has not been achieved at the EPC store. He said Ichi needed to standardize the level of CS and this practice should be shared in any local context to maintain the same brand image of Ichi. While Utada explained that he gave up the bowing part as it might be too much for local employees, Lisa said, "Bowing is just too hard." Utada expected local employees to smile, greet more, and act from the customer's point of view. He then played a DVD that introduced the standard practice of CS in the cash register. In the videotape, a mainland Chinese girl was shown how to provide the Ichi way of service. When local employees found she was from mainland China, they said, "Are you sure the Chinese could able polite like this?" After the videotape was finished, Utada explained the importance of cashiers.

> The last place that customers visit is the cash register, which represents the image of the store. Customers might not be able to find a single staff during their shopping and it might possible that no one helped them in the fitting room. Even though they have a bad shopping experience at the shop floor, if employees behave politely at the cash register by saying, "I am so sorry for keeping you wait. Welcome again" with a smile, I am certain we could at least turn their image to relatively positive in the end. Just imagine that you see Mickey Mouse before you leave the Disneyland! That's pretty exciting, isn't it? (No one has a clear reaction) Anyway, I hope everyone who attended today's meeting could promise me that you would practice CS. My plan is that by April, we can improve CS and try to reduce overtime work. Let's make our store the number one store in Hong Kong!

Utada was very excited when he gave the speech even though he had a stomach ache because of the stress. He had high expectations of the local employees and believed they could gradually change their consciousness. However, I felt local employees could not feel the same as Utada, and fewer of them had the confidence or motivation to achieve such a goal.

Utada was motivated to encourage new full-timers regarding the issue of CS as Utada considered encouraging experienced full-timers who had less motivation to be hopeless. Utada countered the negative influence of experienced employees by continually giving compliments to new full-timers. His conversation with a new Full-time Salesperson, Charles, at the monthly face-to-face meeting will show it clearly. Lisa was likewise present at this occasion but she did not say anything and I played a role of an interpreter.

UTADA: You are a cheerful person and mood-maker. I hope you could continue doing so and pass the same attitude to others in the next step.

CHARLES: I believe I can do better.

UTADA: Just keep working based on the fundamental principles. I count on you. Do you enjoy working at Ichi?

CHARLES: Very happy.

UTADA: When do you feel that way?

CHARLES: People here make me happy.

UTADA: What kind of people?

CHARLES: My colleagues and working environment please me. When I found products the customers asked for, and they would be really thankful. I feel satisfied.

UTADA: Do you like serving customers?

CHARLES: Yes.

UTADA: We, including myself, tend to become '*sagyōin* (manual workers)" over the years without being aware it. You feel satisfied when customers express their appreciation but later on, you might satisfy yourself by finishing the replenishment on time or arranging the layout. These are not bad, but I expect you to remember the fundamentals of the service industry.

During the face-to-face interview, Utada repeatedly emphasized his expectations of Charles and hoped he could become a positive role model in the store. Charles likewise showed his agreement with Utada's claim and told me later that he wanted to develop his skills in the practice of CS as he believed it was one of the major promotional criteria.

Utada not only tried to require experienced full-timers to practice CS, but he encouraged part-timers to do so. For instance, when Utada helped the cashier to pack products, he encouraged local part-timers in English, "Your smile good, hands good.[2] Smile every day, every time!" About this conversation, he explained,

> There is no person who dislikes being praised. Ichi culture tells us to praise staff. It is my job to train Lisa on CS. But it is difficult since her CS is not good. I just want Lisa to realize the importance of the compliment.

Another example is that I once saw Utada compliment the greeting of a local full-timer who was famous for her bad CS. Utada said, "Good greeting! Keep it!" After Utada left, she walked toward me and said that she doubted the sincerity of Utada's compliment and it did not help her to gain more working shifts. Similar to the case of higher-ranked employees, part-timers had the poor motivation to practice CS because of the strong influence of Lisa and the other full-timers.

One month after Utada's arrival at the EPC store, he was relocated to the Tuen Mun store; however, after two months, Utada was relocated to the EPC store. The pressure Utada exerted and overstepping on the duties of James in terms of store operation could have caused the local Store Manager, James to report Utada's behaviors to the Director of the Human Resources Department and state that he could not work with Utada anymore. James had a relatively strong voice in Hong Kong as he was one of the more experienced Store Managers. I will not further discuss Utada's relations with local employees at the Tuen Mun store due to the limited data.

After being sent back to the EPC store, Utada was disappointed with their attitude of James and was worried that Utada's management style was wrong. Similarly, he assumed he could be sent back to Japan. Soon after his return to the EPC store, he found Lisa had focused on the practice of CS and believed his efforts had paid off. Utada once said to me,

> Lisa is doing her best these days. I saw her ask employees to recite the "Six Magic Words" and greeting again and again when they failed to achieve the standard. Although Hong Kong people do not have a habit of bowing, Store Managers do so in the meeting at the Head Office. Lisa has recently required employees to recite the "Six Magic Words" at least three times. When she finds they bow in different speeds or their voices are not loud enough, she asks them to repeat these practices. At the very beginning, they were not standardized, but through a number of repeats several employees have improved considerably.

In August 2011, after five months of work in Hong Kong, an announcement was made, stating that Utada and another Japanese Store Manager were to return to Japan. For the first half-year assessment, five Japanese Store Managers "survived." According to another Store Manager, Nakamura, Utada was highly evaluated by Mizuno in his early days at the EPC store because he could practice what the company expected. Moreover, his relocation to the Tuen Mun store was based on his positive evaluation and the situation was relatively stable at the EPC store. However, this relocation turned out to be the major reason for his back to Japan. Utada's wife was very shocked by the assessment and commented that she could never trust anyone again because she felt it was unfair and that her husband was not evaluated properly.

After Utada left, several local employees at the EPC store shared their feelings with me. The security man who came from mainland China said,

> That Japanese man has left. That day, he came to me and said something. I guess he said something like, 'Thank you' and 'You are good'. The Japanese are normally very polite to people and he had a mild temper.

The local Store Manager, Lisa, commented that although Utada was a nice guy, she learned nothing from him because of his poor knowledge of the local situation.

There were several reasons why Utada was not able to achieve his goal: to change the interpretation of CS by local employees. First and most importantly, he did not have "actual" power over the human resources issue in Hong Kong. From local employees' points of view, even if Utada had evaluated highly their work performances, it might not directly link to their future promotion. This was further stressed by the reluctant attitude of the Store Manager who had "actual" power. Second, the limited time for the assessment gave him strong pressure to achieve the goal. Utada went stepped on the scope of authority of the local Store Manager, James could have been caused by Utada's enthusiastic sense of responsibility and belief in the necessity of changing the fundamental ideology of local employees to improve the practice of CS. Third, his poor language skills and poor knowledge of the local store operation prevented him from building his authority within the store. He could not respond to the customers' requests without being helped by other employees and his ignorance toward the local operation has likewise damaged his image at the store.

The next regime I am going to analyze paints quite a different picture from Utada in the sense that the latter avoided public conflict by maintaining stable relations with local employees.

Nakamura Regime: Adaptive Attitudes

A distinctive feature of the regime of the Japanese Store Manager, Nakamura, was that while he maintained *aikata* (partner) relationship with the local Store Managers, he likewise maintained a stable relationship with subordinates exhibiting his status as a supporter rather than a trainer or Store Manager. He required less CS from local employees compared to Utada and Nakamura did not neglect the issue of sales. These practices were aimed to contribute to his goal, which was to pass the half-year assessment.

Nakamura was from the Kansai area and sometimes spoke a Kansai accent, which was similar to another Japanese Store Manager, Kaneko, who was from Osaka. He was the second youngest Store Manager among the seven Japanese managers who were sent to Hong Kong in early 2011. His parents and grandparents owned their shops while his young brother went to Australia for future career development. Nakamura had little interest in running his parents' business in the future but to start his own business in the near future because he was bad at playing up to bosses. Before graduation, he had applied to numerous companies, but most had rejected his application.

Although he got an offer from a large firm, he could not bear the idea of having to follow the supervisor for the first three years. Ichi suited him because the company offered more freedom to candidates who could be promoted to Store Manager faster than in other retailers. Most importantly, he could actually feel that he was "working." He described his career path as tough because he was demoted during the Store Manager period, and this event strongly influenced his career path.

Nakamura worked at the Plaza Hollywood store in Hong Kong for the first half-year in 2011 and then he was relocated to manage the City Plaza store and EPC store at the same time for another half-year. Data on Nakamura were based mainly on my three months of working at the City Plaza store.

Nakamura had a clear goal that he needed to improve CS and increase sales. He changed his focus according to the different agenda. For instance, when Nakamura was working at the Plaza Hollywood and City Plaza stores, he focused on the level of CS because of lower results. The reason he emphasized the improvement of the level of CS was because he believed the lower level indicated poor employee satisfaction. He did not neglect the factor of sales and thus, they would sometimes skip the morning briefing or store meeting to replenish the stock. Different from Utada, he acted more as an independent worker and sometimes arranged the shop floor according to his own idea without reporting to the local Store Manager in advance although he did not go beyond their authority.

Local Store Manager as Aikata (Partner)

Nakamura changed his attitude based on the different characteristics of the local Store Manager. In general, he kept "*aikata*" (partner) relationship with the local Store Manager to gain their trust except in the case of Yu who was assigned to the EPC store after Lisa.

Nakamura was first assigned to the Plaza Hollywood store to teach the local junior Store Manager, Tsui, who started her career from the bottom of the hierarchy. Plaza Hollywood store was the smallest store in Hong Kong and was located in a shopping mall near the Diamond Hill metro station. Unlike the shopping mall in Kowloon Tung or Harbor City, this shopping mall provided relatively lower-end brands. The Ichi store in Plaza Hollywood was surrounded by local fashion retailers. Nakamura felt happy to be assigned to such a small store because he believed it might be better for him to build relationships with local employees.

After passing the half-year evaluation for Japanese Store Managers, Nakamura was assigned to the EPC and City Plaza stores. While the EPC store had average total sales, the City Plaza store was regarded as a significant store with high sales. Mizuno expected him to reconstruct the working environment of the EPC store and help the junior Store Manager at the City Plaza store. Although Nakamura was assigned to two stores, he spent most of the time at the City Plaza store. His limited visits to the EPC store due to the stability of the store and the reluctance of the Store Manager, Yu, who came after Lisa. Although Nakamura supported most local Store Managers, he tended to interact less with Yu who happened to work with Kaneko, another Japanese Store Manager at the New Town Plaza store before the relocation. Although Yu had relatively long years of service at Ichi, her reluctant attitude toward work was famous among local Store Managers. Japanese Store Managers had likewise heard of this characteristic of Kaneko. After working with Yu, Nakamura confirmed this rumor. It was a tricky problem for the EPC store; however, because of the relatively stable labor force at the EPC store, Nakamura focused more on the City Plaza store.

In the following section, I shall examine how Nakamura used his poor language ability to pretend he lowered his status and hide his existence at the store by attempting to observe the "real" daily operations to better interact with local employees.

Support Subordinates

Nakamura interacted with a wide range of employees using his poor English, especially at the City Plaza where he worked most of the time. Nakamura's limited English sometimes compelled him to use Japanese with gestures to convey his message to local employees. Even though his English was poor, Nakamura tried to communicate with local employees as much as possible. Moreover, he regarded himself as more or less a partner (*aikata*) of the local Store Manager rather than the trainer. As time went on, it was quite interesting to find several local employees talking with Nakamura in Japanese, especially several special Ichi terms, such as "*tettei* (thoroughness)," "*kijyun* (standard)," and so on. They would sometimes even say "*dame*" (not good) directly to Nakamura to evaluate his performance, which he appeared to care less. This attitude might have contributed to him building a closer relationship with local employees as several Japanese Store Managers tended to care too much about how local employees perceived them and whether local employees said bad things about them, which might result in less communication. Nakamura commented that even though he cannot understand well what local employees were talking about, he did not find any problem communicating with them.

In addition to direct communication, he even "hides" his existence to observe their daily operations and discover the real problems. If we compare the different attitudes of local employees during Nakamura's speech in the morning briefing session at the EPC and City Plaza stores, we can find the understanding toward Nakamura differed.

I shall first introduce the case at the EPC store. The briefing session was about to start at the EPC store and everyone stood in front of the cash registers at 10:30 am. A Senior Salesperson asked an Advanced Salesperson standing next to him, "Do we have to wait for Nakamura-san to come?" He said, "No need." Ten minutes to Eleven, Nakamura joined our session and gave his speech in English. In the first part of his speech, he complimented the performance of employees such as the organized Back Room. He then showed his expectation toward employee communication and eye contact with customers. Nakamura only spoke two to three sentences at each point. Although he had a strong Japanese accent, I could understand what he was saying. However, a full-timer said to me, "You could translate for us." Then a part-timer said, "I actually could not understand a word he said." A few of them expressed the same idea. After my translation, the Senior Salesperson said in front of all staff, "Today, we have a Japanese Store Manager with us; thus, we need to do better. Otherwise, he would have a negative image of us, which would influence your evaluation."

A different response was seen at the City Plaza store. During a briefing session before the opening of the store Nakamura and I attended in the City Plaza store, he made comment on the store's high sales and highly evaluated the level of CS using English and some Japanese terms. Although he was not able to speak English in one sentence, I basically understood his meaning. However, the faces of most local employees showed their confusion. I thought I might be asked to translate; however, I soon heard a local Senior Salesperson translate his idea to Cantonese correctly. That Senior Salesperson had not studied Japanese before; however, after working with Nakamura for some time, she could guess what he wanted to convey. In addition to the Senior Salesperson, the Store Manager could gain a general idea of his message. Moreover, full-timers were not very aware of Nakamura's presence as they found it quite natural to see him.

The above description indicates that the EPC store employees, especially higher-ranked employees were sensitive to Nakamura's presence and wanted to show a "presentation of self". Employees at the City Plaza store were largely unconcerned with Nakamura's presence and employees who frequently worked with him understood what he attempted to convey. This difference has occurred because of Nakamura's limited visits to the EPC store and employees with different interpretations of Japanese Store Managers.

Similar to the case of Utada, Nakamura also used e-mail to share his ideas with higher-ranked employees at the City Plaza store. Nakamura first expressed his expectations for the promotion of local employees and then announced the next week's sales plan, and finally, he pointed out the lower level of customer satisfaction. Through numerous gatherings with Nakamura, I could feel he understood the strong hope of local employees toward their promotional opportunities and likewise understood that some local employees had difficulties in improving their level of CS even though they worked hard.

> First, I really hope our staff who worked hard could be promoted next month. Please provide feedback and educate those candidates. This is very important. If they cannot be promoted, it would be because of the Store Manager. I shall share the next week's planning with you.

> Our stores did not win the CS award this month. We would like to evaluate employees who worked hard. Please educate those candidates. Both of their CS levels are quite high. The significant point is training them. Please do so, starting from the person in charge.

While Nakamura emphasized the importance of subordinate training, he believed the result of CS checkup was dependent on the performance of specific employees during particular dates. Therefore, he spent less time pressuring local employees to practice CS because he believed training was more important as it allowed local employees to learn from behavior. Although Nakamura rarely required them to practice CS, he in fact could not understand the different divisions of labor in Hong Kong. When I invited him to come to the University for a lecture, he asked students a question about something that had confused him for a long time. He asked, "Why do so many people not want to pick up the trash and leave it for the cleaners to handle? Why don't people respect cleaning employees?" A male student answered it was because of the difference in the division of labor. Nakamura still could understand and asked me about it after the lecture. Although I explained that some differences in the terms of the job assignment and labor structure between Hong Kong and Japan existed, Nakamura still believed every staff person should pick up the trash when it was necessary. However, I rarely saw him ask local Ichi employees this question or require them to pick up the trash.

Although Nakamura and Utada shared ethnic backgrounds, the former was different from the latter in terms of his approach toward local employees and his management. Nakamura paid attention to both CS and sales issues, he required fewer local employees to practice CS. Moreover, he adapted his attitude toward different local Store Managers flexibly and he spent the most time interacting with a wide range of employees in an attempt to build trust relationships. He was able to observe the "true" operations by lowering his status as a Japanese Store Manager. The Japanese Store Manager in the next regime also emphasized both CS and sales issues, his management style resulted in his detachment from the local Store Managers.

Kaneko Regime: Detached Relations

Kaneko Regime was represented by the characteristic of his limited interaction with two local Store Managers, Yu and Lisa, at the New Town Plaza store where he worked for one year. Although Kaneko was reluctant to build a relationship with the local Store Manager, he was able to pass the first half-year assessment because his stable relationship with subordinates allowed him to gain cooperation from subordinates, which helped the store gain an A-grade in the CS checkup in the first half-year.

Kaneko was from Osaka, Kansai area. After graduating from the university in Hokkaido, Kaneko entered Ichi in 1999. In the next year, he was promoted to Store Manager. After four years, Kaneko was promoted to Store Manager

(S3). Kaneko was relocated to several places, mainly in Kansai Area, and was transferred to Hong Kong in 2011. He and his wife have three children and all of them accompanied him to Hong Kong, which was a rare case in Ichi. Mizuno discouraged him to bring all his family members to Hong Kong since some Japanese wives found it difficult to adapt to the local environment. Kaneko's wife insisted on coming to Hong Kong with her husband and they ended up living in Fo Tan, which is located north of Kowloon Island. Compared with other Japanese Store Managers, his apartment, which had three bedrooms, cost the company the most.

From March 2011 to February 2011, Kaneko worked at the New Town Plaza Store in Shatin. In the first half a year, he worked with the Store Manager Yu and then he worked with the Store Manager Lisa. It is interesting to note that Yu later worked with Nakamura and Lisa used to work with Utada. Therefore, Kaneko gave much information to Nakamura before Yu's relocation and Kaneko had already heard a lot about Lisa from Utada.

During Kaneko's first half a year in Hong Kong, he tended to work by himself rather than educating the local Store Manager, Yu. Kaneko was frequently upset by their lower work motivation and job performance of Yu and whenever the Japanese Store Manager shared their experiences with local Store Managers, he emphasized that she was an exceptionally unqualified Store Manager.

KANEKO: After she arrived at the store in the morning, she checked the money and '*ijyō taiten hokoku* (abnormal closure report)' briefly without filing the documents, which was necessary. When I expected her to check the shop floor, she just gave the person in charge instructions for about 30 minutes and then arranged the daily work schedule. Finally, she came out of the higher-ranked employees room and checked the shop floor for about 30 minutes.

UTADA: Isn't the shop floor checkup usually conducted after the opening?

KANEKO: Because after the opening, it was time for her to rest. When I wrote down many mistakes in the shop floor checkup sheet, she only wrote two because the person in charge had done most of the time. The person in charge received zero feedback from her. In addition to the absence of feedback for the shop floor checkup, she likewise did not provide feedback for the replenishment plan. She merely signed the papers. Honestly, she did nothing. Thus, I can only work by myself without her. I actually intentionally worked separately from her. I can work better without her.

In addition to their lower job motivation of Yu, Kaneko likewise criticized her lower level of CS. He stated that the level of the Store Manager Yu was the lowest and Full-time Salespersons had the highest level of CS at his store. Kaneko stated that other store employees were influenced negatively by Yu's lower motivation and performance.

KANEKO: Every staff noticed that she never worked. Other Store Managers might help in the replenishment of the shop floor, but they had never seen Yu replenish the stock with them. Moreover, no one saw her fold clothes. Even on the shop floor, she seemed less energetic.

NAKAMURA: Isn't that something?

UTADA: Didn't she even say "Thank you for coming" to customers on the shop floor?

KANEKO: No. I once asked her to say so and she followed. But her voice was one-tenth of that of other employees. Everybody hates her.

NAKAMURA: Your store must die in the CS checkup.

KANEKO: Definitely. Our store obtained the A-rank last time because of my work. If I am not around, the result might be B or C.

UTADA: You set her a high bar.

KANEKO: If things do not go well, we might get D-rank. In such case, I would definitely be accused of poor work by Mizuno-san. I believe employees could achieve higher level of CS; however, they do not know how to achieve it. If I stand in the shop floor, everything is different. I usually observe the entire store from the entrance and record videos through my i-Phone and walk around the store, asking employees to make their improvement.

Kaneko emphasized his contribution to the store and his case was similar to that of Utada in terms of their enthusiasm toward store improvement. However, Yu was not as aggressive as James, the local Store Manager at the Tuen Mun store. Yu simply wanted to maintain her current status rather than pursue a higher rank at Ichi. Although Yu was aware that Kaneko threatened her authority, she tried to take credit for Kaneko's effort as her own. For instance, after the A-grade CS checkup result came out, Yu emphasized that the result was through her efforts. She claimed she conducted a series of reforms that allowed the store to gain such results. However, Kaneko knew that Yu did not do anything but only stayed in the staff room. Although the Head Office higher-ranked employees had heard from Kaneko regarding their reluctant work attitude of Yu in advance, Yu did not change her claim.

Even though Kaneko observed Yu was changing in a positive direction, Kaneko wanted her to be relocated so he could dedicate himself fully to store management as a "real" Store Manager. While Kaneko criticized Yu, he claimed subordinates, especially higher-ranked employees who were assigned numerous work tasks, complained about Yu's work performance. Most the higher-ranked employees began their career when the Japanese Store Manager still worked at the New Town Plaza and their job skills were quite high. Kaneko gained support from subordinates because he trained subordinates and managed the store operation instead of Yu, which contributed largely to the A-grade of CS checkup.

Kaneko passed the first half-year assessment because of the continuous higher annual sales of the store, which was in fact common in Ichi stores in Hong Kong, and the dramatic changes as a result of the CS checkup. His relatively positive relationship with subordinates allowed him to gain their support in terms of the 'collaborative' practice of CS.

Kaneko continued with a similar strategy after Lisa who used to work with Utada was relocated from the EPC store. Unlike Yu, Lisa worked harder than most employees and had a clear image of the replenishment plan and floor layout. Moreover, she preferred to create a general plan by herself, one which she checked every time.

Although Kaneko's authority was reduced, he soon found Lisa interacted less with subordinates, which allowed Kaneko to maintain a stable relationship with them. Kaneko commented that Lisa cared less about subordinate training.

> I do not agree with the Utada's high evaluation of Lisa. Although she did good job of finding mistakes in the shop floor, she spent less time training subordinates. For instance, several employees made the same mistakes again and again. Lisa usually cleaned it up by herself. Even though I told Lisa to educate them, she just says, "Ah" and then leaves during our conversation. When she corrected mistakes, I thought she was educating them; but instead, she scolded them. I found new employees felt close to Lisa but several senior employees were not because no matter how lazy the previous Store Manager, Yu, was, she had a clear distinction between her personal life and work. However, Lisa's work attitude to some extent negatively influenced their motivation towards promotion. Recently, a male Assistant Store Manager was expected to take the examinations for Deputy Store Manager, but he was less motivated after working with Lisa. In this sense, Yu might be better for their career path.

Kaneko pointed out Lisa's shortcomings and tried to encourage her to train subordinates but he likewise failed to do so similar to Utada. Therefore, Kaneko took the responsibility of educating subordinates, which allowed him to spend more time with the local employees. In contrast with Nakamura, Kaneko paid more attention to directly training subordinates rather than simply supporting them.

Kaneko's regime was represented by his detachment from two local Store Managers; however, he was able to gain support from local subordinates for achieving a better result for two reasons. First, many local subordinates had a similar interpretation of the local Store Manager as Kaneko and expected more from Kaneko rather than the local Store Manager. Second, Kaneko "showed" his authority as a Store Manager rather than a trainer although his power over the human resources issue was limited. Although both Utada and Kaneko worked with Lisa, human relations within their regimes differed mainly because Utada failed to demonstrate his power and focused too much on the issue of CS to which the local employees paid little attention.

Conclusion

In this chapter, I have examined five different regimes to show how the career orientations of Store Managers and their different interpretations of the corporate ideology have transformed worker relations.

Store Managers had two types of career orientations including aggressive and reluctant, and interpreted the core principles of the corporate ideology – increasing sales and improving the practice of CS – differently to meet their career goals. Only Jenny was categorized into the reluctant orientation and she used CS practice as her major tool to secure her current position. Four other Store Managers, including Lisa, Utada, Nakamura, and Kaneko were categorized into aggressive orientation in the sense that they all pursued promotion or, in the case of the Japanese, passed half a year's assessment. By examining different interpretations of corporate ideology, I found that it is the interpretation of corporate ideology that has influenced Store Managers' behaviors rather than their ethnic background.

Human relations during the Jenny regime were largely influenced by her reluctant attitude toward promotion although she still wanted to keep her current position within the company. The major strategy Jenny used to achieve this goal was to focus on the practice of CS to highlight her work performance to the company by neglecting other aspects, such as subordinate training and increasing sales. Human relations during Jenny's regime had two distinctive features. Although subordinates displayed "harmonious" relations, the implicit conflict between subordinates and Store Managers existed. The second feature was Jenny's reluctant attitude and the poor job skills of some higher-ranked employees; thus, the male Senior Salesperson was able to gain stronger authority and higher status on the shop floor than employees who ranked higher than him.

Lisa was aggressive on the issues of sales but neglected the practice of CS and human relations within the store because she believed the former factor was a major concern of the company and an important promotion criterion. Worker interaction during Lisa's regime was represented by two characteristics. Subordinates were detached from the Store Manager because of Lisa's over-emphasis on sales rather than human relations. At the same time, they were highly motivated because Lisa strongly supported subordinate promotion. However, along with the increase in worker motivation, the power of the Senior Salesperson was limited. Moreover, public conflict occurred among full-timers because everyone focused on their tasks assigned by Lisa to achieve future promotion rather than cooperating with each other.

Utada focused on the improvement of CS by attempting to change the fundamental consciousness of employees because he believed this strategy was beneficial to the creation of a customer-first store, which is one of the major promotional criteria. At the EPC store, subordinates, especially higher-ranked employees including the local Store Manager, displayed a cooperative attitude toward Utada although they were reluctant to practice his suggestions since local employees followed more on Lisa who placed little emphasis on CS and who had actual power over human resources issues. At the Tuen Mun store, the conflict between the male local Store Manager and Utada was fierce and apparent because Utada's work performance overstepped the authority of the local Store Manager.

Nakamura understood that both the growth rate in sales and the level of CS were significant for his assessment and future career development in Ichi. He used his poor English skills and easygoing personality to less emphasize his status at the store. Moreover, unlike "typical" Japanese expatriates from the local's point of view, Nakamura did not strongly require employees to practice CS. In Nakamura's regime, he maintained an "*aikata*" (partner) relationship with the local Store Managers while using the employee-first attitude with subordinates to maintain a stable relationship.

Kaneko emphasized sales and the practice of CS similar to Nakamura. However, to achieve this goal, Kaneko neglected the presence of the local Store Manager who was an obstacle to achieving his goals. This neglect resulted in their detachment. Kaneko played the role of a "real" Store Manager rather than simply a trainer and directly trained subordinates himself. His behavior did not result in public conflict or even a complaint from the first Store Manager, Yu, because she merely wanted to secure her current position without having any trouble. Lisa who was more ambitious had less public conflict with Kaneko since Kaneko did not interrupt her job but took care of the issue of the practice of CS.

As the above description, Store Managers play the role as the "soul" of the company who could determine the store atmosphere, subordinates' work performance, and even human relations. Moreover, by examining the actions of different nationalities, the book also shows that Store Managers manage human relations within their stores primarily on the basis of different interpretations of the corporate ideology rather than their ethnic backgrounds.

The significant presence of Store Managers is also supported by the design of the company structure, which allows Store Managers to have a certain degree of autonomy. Moreover, the company trains Store Managers to become ultimate multifunctional workers whose bonus and promotion depend on their skills in gaining support from subordinates.

Notes

1 Unique *shoten* (shop) is the word used by the Japanese Operations Manager to describe the uniqueness of Lisa's management style which did not strictly follow the Ichi-style.

2 Cashier has to wave their hands to show customers the availability of the cash register.

References

Kezar, A. (2013) Understanding Sensemaking/Sensegiving in Transformational Change Processes from the Bottom Up. *Higher Education*, 65(6), pp. 761–780.

Maitlis, S. (2005) The Social Processes of Organizational Sensemaking. *The Academy of Management Journal*, 48(1), pp. 21–49.

Mills, J.H., Thurlow, A., & Mills, A.J. (2010) Making Sense of Sensemaking: The Critical Sensemaking Approach. *Qualitative Research in Organizations and Management: An International Journal,* 5, pp. 182–195.

Weick, K.E. (1995) *Sensemaking in Organizations (Vol. 3).* London: Sage.

9 Becoming a Real Global Company

This book describes a Japanese fashion company's building process by examining how the company formed and expressed its distinctive ideology and how employees' various interpretations of this ideology created unique human relationships.

To develop the organization, Ichi identified, defined, and then refined its ideology, "Ichi DNA," based on historical business practices and the founder's legacy. The term "DNA" refers to the genetic nature and traits of an organism that are inherited and cannot be changed. In the case of Ichi, "DNA" is used to refer to the company's ideology that employees could "inherit," thereby helping to form the genetic identity of the company. The core principle of Ichi's corporate ideology focuses on globalization, under a policy known as "Global One," which aims to standardize the Ichi DNA worldwide.

By analyzing Ichi's operations in Hong Kong, I found that the company has steadily upheld its corporate image in the local market by stressing requirements such as customer satisfaction (CS) and Ichi standards. To develop the organization smoothly, Ichi relied on Store Managers to play the role of "missionaries," spreading the Ichi DNA in Hong Kong. Ichi's organizational structure, to some extent, protected the autonomy and independence of Store Managers, who were given strong decision-making powers and authority over subordinates. Moreover, superiors from the Head Office rarely intervened in Store Managers' decisions because of a detached office-store relationship. This detachment made it impossible for Ichi to implement its DNA ideology equally in every store at the same time, requiring the company to use an informal hierarchy to determine which stores received priority and became "models" for the implementation of Ichi DNA.

Ichi's corporate system of training, ranking, remuneration, and promotion is based on its corporate ideology, and the book shows how the company encouraged employees to learn Ichi-specific skills and monitored their performance in incorporating these skills to develop the organization. Through its unique corporate system, Ichi planned to generate a critical mass of DNA holders who would accelerate the development of the organization.

During the implementation of its corporate ideology, employees have various interpretations of corporate ideology. When employees shared their

DOI: 10.4324/9781003305675-9

individual interpretations of the corporate ideology, a phenomenon referred to as the "presentation of self" became apparent. The extent of the "presentation of self" expanded from the individual to the collective level as more employees shared their interpretations and goals. Manipulation of certain groups in terms of their interpretation of company ideology became particularly apparent when Ichi evaluated employees at a store where evaluators were not familiar with staff members. These staff members were found to be "easier" to manipulate than others.

In order to understand how different interpretations of the corporate ideology transformed human interactions I examined groups of five Store Managers, with two local higher-ranked employees and three Japanese managers in each group, to reveal how each determined store atmosphere and human interactions. The examination of five Store Managers with different nationalities illustrates that it is not ethnicity but the interpretation of company ideology that is the driving factor behind the creation of different store structures.

Implications of the Study

My detailed ethnographic analysis of conflicts and manipulation during Ichi's organizational development process has the following implications: First, the findings challenge conventional ideas held by many Japanologists, who confuse corporate ideology with its actual practice. Japanologists claim that the distinctive feature of the Japanese company is its cultural influence. Japanologists stress that while a Japanese company is typically represented by its "familialism," Japanese employees' behavior is based on harmony, consensus, collectivism, and so on. Ichi de-emphasized this attachment to employees and instead focused on whether employees learned the Ichi DNA ideology. Whenever Ichi's founder appeared in interviews, he suggested that the company preferred to hire people based on capability rather than merely hiring people who were more likely to stay with the company for the rest of their lives. This philosophy is borne out in Ichi's corporate ideology. It is interesting to note that promotion through Ichi's ranks requires employees to become mutually dependent on one another, because assessments are based, in part, on the performance of their colleagues. Rather than so-called familialism, Ichi expected that this practice would result in enhancing teamwork and increasing the loyalty of employees toward the company as a whole, thereby leading to greater efficiency.

As regards the employees, both Japanese and local employees were found to embody the values of harmonious and collective performance. Data from the previous chapters reveal how local employees in Hong Kong performed "harmoniously" and "collaboratively" when they shared the same goals and similar interpretations of the corporate ideology. This indicates that employees understood the kind of performance that was expected from them and grasped the key criteria for receiving promotions. This paved the way for effective collaboration between employees, which was used to manipulate the impressions and evaluations made by superiors. My analysis found that this type of collaboration was rarely observed in the day-to-day operations of the company, and only occurred during assessment periods.

This underscores that external appearances at Ichi might not reveal the complete picture. However, many management scholars or Japanologists have focused on Japanese companies' external cultural forms and neglected the substance behind the form. Even when answering questionnaires, or in face-to-face interviews, employees would manipulate their answers or conversations, whether unintentionally or intentionally, although the extent of this would differ from case to case. Therefore, this book suggests that long-term fieldwork on-site is crucial for researchers to understand the real picture of the company.

Second, we could not interpret the power of corporate ideology over human interactions and managerial control as a total absolute, meaning that the implementation of Ichi's corporate ideology does not always result in the ideology becoming ingrained or "unquestionable" in the minds of its employees. As Wong (1999: 199) describes, "Power is culturally mediated and thus has differential effects on different groups of people" so it is important not to over-emphasize the role of power but to consider that it is transmitted through culture and is different in different cultural contexts. In addition to the influence of corporate ideology, we must look into how conflicts of interest among employees have influenced the company's managerial practices, and record these findings.

Ichi believed that "packing" the successful business model with its Ichi-specific ideology and standardizing it in all markets would allow the company to replicate its success. However, the case of Ichi in Hong Kong shows that internal politics among employees have an even greater influence on the efficacy of particular management policies or regulations than the company's rationally designed system. Many employee cases show that because of the fluidity of their interests, they might collaborate for one minute and in the next, they might change their minds and cease to cooperate. This gap between personal agendas and corporate ideology shows us that we cannot rely on remote observations to examine institutional culture and neglect to pay attention to what is happening on-site.

This book also sheds light on the significance of the local context in the organizational development process and points out the limitations of "scientific management." This examination of Ichi's logically designed corporate system has resulted in different outcomes in Hong Kong and Japan, and at times, has even caused inefficiencies. This illustrates the inefficacy of the theory of the "Universalists" who believe that an overarching formula for success can be applied in any company in any location. Besides worker politics, external factors such as economic background and the local labor market must be considered seriously.

Third, this book questions the argument of Japanese management as ethnocentric since it is not ethnicity but the interpretation of corporate ideology that has influenced managerial practice and employee behaviors. Shared ethnic backgrounds mattered little in this case since it includes two Japanese Store Managers whose interpretations of corporate ideology, career orientation, approach to managerial control, and relations with local employees were different. At the same time, Store Managers with different ethnic backgrounds shared identical interpretations of corporate ideology, even though the data show that their means of control and goals differed. Therefore, there was no absolute relationship between the ethnic background of Store Managers and their managerial practices.

Scholars in management studies have identified Japanese companies overseas as ethnocentric based on the fact that they selected disproportionately more Japanese people than local employees for higher management positions (such as Kopp, 1994; Legewie, 2000; Seki and Han, 2003; Yahagi, 2007). This argument is untenable since it neglects the company's goal of building its "empire" using corporate ideology. It was therefore not ethnicity but skills that led to the selection of Japanese managers. For instance, the CEO of Ichi Hong Kong, Zhang Peng, was from mainland China. Although it can be argued that this assignment would help Ichi promote its image as a global company, more importantly, Zhang was believed to possess "Ichi DNA." The number of Japanese superiors indicates that there were insufficient local employees who possessed "Ichi DNA." This does not mean that local employees were not willing to learn Ichi skills. This paper provides a picture of how local employees were motivated to "voluntarily" manipulate their work performance to demonstrate qualifications that facilitated career development.

After his long-term observation of the Japanese megastore Fumei, Wong (1999) also argued that Japanese employees have used their ethnic superiority to distinguish themselves from local employees. Therefore, we could not ignore the fact that some companies do use ethnocentric ideology in management decisions regarding employees. This is less prevalent at Ichi, mainly because of its unique historical development, economic environment, and the founder's legacy. Fumei was established before World War II, and the economic situation at that time was quite different from when Ichi was established in 1984. The historic and economic climate in Japan at these times influenced the personal traits of both founders. Although both founders had strong ambitions toward globalization, Ichi preferred the more "scientific" western approach to management although he admired both western and Japanese management philosophies. Moreover, the global economy was vastly different from the time of Fumei, when Ichi ventured abroad. The flow of goods, services, and capital had greatly increased by the time of Ichi's overseas expansion, and business practices had changed due to the penetration of the Internet and the popularity of the smartphone. These internal and external factors prompted differing management decisions and practices.

Evidence found in this book suggests that Store Mangers' interpretation of corporate ideology can change according to internal and external factors. One local Store Manager, Lisa, who placed a great emphasis on sales during her first several months, started to put more effort into CS since she believed that CS was also an important factor for her future promotion, even though she gave importance to sales since she interpreted it as the company's real goal. Although some scholars claim that Japanese society is characterized by a group model that creates an absolute Japanese "self" (Hasegawa and Hirose, 2005), others claim that it is relational and fluid (Araki, 1973; Bachnik, 1992; Kondo, 1990). I echo the latter argument and add that it might not be limited to the situation in Japan but may also apply in Hong Kong in the sense that local employees also adjust their "self" on various occasions during negotiations with one another.

Future Viability of Ichi DNA

This book reveals that although Ichi paid much effort to implement its corporate ideology in Hong Kong so as to develop its organization in an overseas market (by gaining a critical mass of Ichi "DNA holders"), the company has not yet achieved the goal of "naturalization" by turning Ichi DNA into something employees "possess." Data from my fieldwork do not provide a clear picture of organizational development in the future, since Ichi constantly changes in response to both internal and external factors.

In the future, Ichi DNA might itself be changed along with an increase in overseas markets. One of the most apparent changes so far is in the company's talent pool. Ichi has paid more attention to global talent acquisitions, along with many other Japanese companies, to gain skillful employees who could also work abroad. To attract more talented people, the company publicized its overseas expansion and the opportunity to work abroad. Because of the recession, an increasing number of young Japanese are reluctant to participate in "traditional" Japanese management, including seniority-based salary and lifetime employment. Many are motivated to prove their abilities as soon as possible and change industries more frequently. Because of the recession, some of these young professionals are attracted to the "Western" style of management since they believed that such companies pay for performance and can offer rapid promotions. Ichi also welcomed more foreign university graduates to join the company, as part of its globalization initiative. This would increase competition among employees, who would be evaluated based on their success in inculcating the "Ichi DNA," as this book has suggested.

We can already observe changes along these lines in Ichi Hong Kong. Through my follow-up interviews and observations after my fieldwork in Hong Kong, I found that the role of university graduates was increasingly emphasized since Ichi believed that they were more "approachable" in terms of the inheritance of DNA compared with employees who had worked in other industries or companies. Besides the "purity" of university graduates, they are younger than current Store Managers and are more ambitious. As the company's focus on the promotion of university graduates continues, the whole face of Ichi might change. During my fieldwork, almost half of the local Store Managers were female and they were either married or had marriage plans. These characteristics have influenced their reluctance to be career orientated. If most Store Managers were replaced by the younger, hungrier generation, Ichi's organizational development process might greatly accelerate in the future since probably, those university graduates have learned how to "better" manipulate the company.

Ichi, similar to many other Japanese companies, will continuously change its corporate ideology according to changing economic factors to survive. Employees will constantly change their interpretation of corporate ideology based on their immediate interests. As Paul Noguchi states, "Organizations are the unique products of cultural and historical events and hence are more than just rational structures" (1990: 193).

References

Araki, H. (1973) *Nihonjin no kōdoyoshiki. [Behavioral Patterns of Japanese]* Tokyo: Kodansha.

Bachnik, J.M. (1989) Omote/Ura: Indexes and the Organization of Self and Society in Japan. *Comparative Social Research*, 11, pp. 239–262.

Hasegawa, Y., & Hirose, Y. (2005) What the Japanese Language Tells Us about the Alleged Japanese Relational Self. *Australian Journal of Linguistics*, 25(2), pp. 219–251.

Kondo, D.K. (1990) *Crafting Selves: Power, Gender and Discourses of Identity in a Japanese Workplace.* Chicago: The University of Chicago Press.

Kopp, R. (1994) *The Rice-Paper Ceiling: Breaking through Japanese Corporate Culture.* Berkeley, CA: Stone Bridge Press.

Legewie, J. (2000) Production Strategies of Japanese Firms: Building Up a Regional Production Network. In Legewie, J. and Meyer-Ohle, H. (eds.), *Corporate Strategies for Southeast Asia after the Crisis*, pp. 74–99. Basingstoke: Palgrave.

Noguchi, P.H. (1990) *Delayed Departures, Overdue Arrivals: Industrial Familiarism and the Japanese National Railway.* Hawaii: University of Hawaii Press.

Seki, M., & Han, K. (eds.) (2003) *Genchika suru chūgoku shinshutsu kigyō [Localization by Japanese Companies in China].* Tokyo: Shinhyoron.

Wong, H.W. (1999) *Japanese Bosses, Chinese Workers: Power and Control in a Hong Kong Megastore.* Richmond, VA: Curzon Press.

Yahagi, T. (2007) *Kouri kokusaika purosesu: Riron to kēsu de kangaeru [Globalization Process of Retailers: Theories and Case Studies].* Tokyo: Yuhikaku.

Index

Note: **Bold** page numbers refer to tables; *Italic* page numbers refer to figures and page numbers followed by "n" denote endnotes.